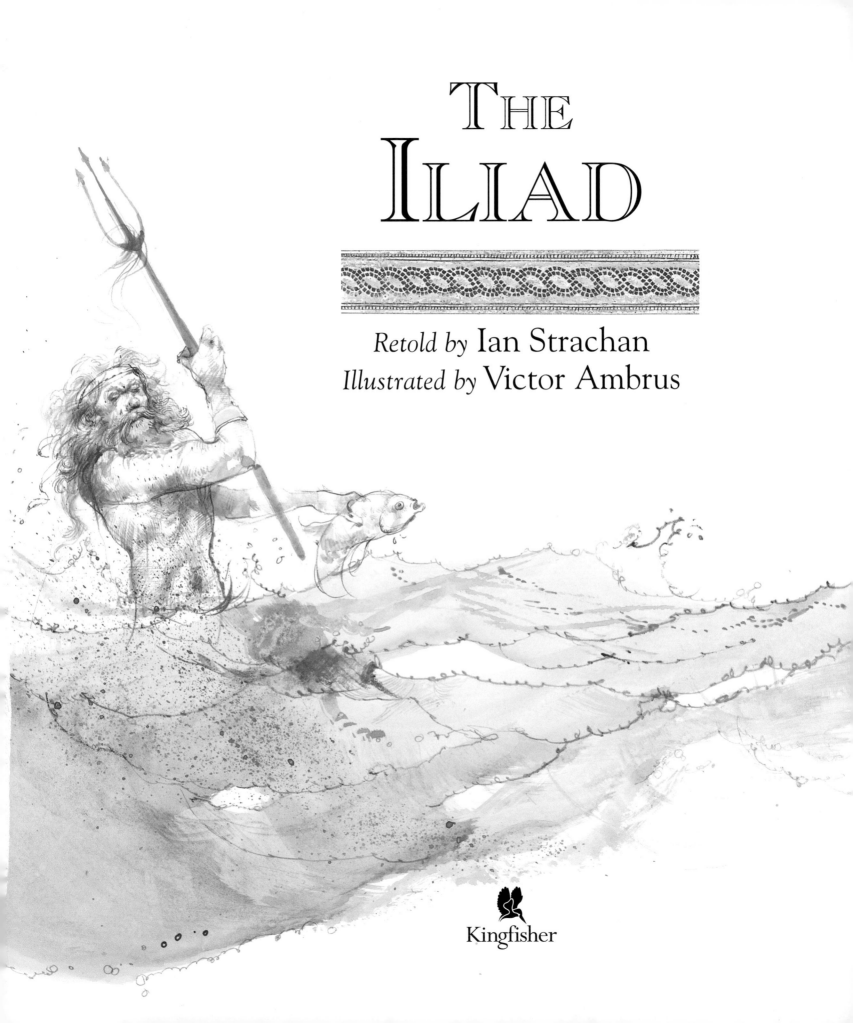

THE ILIAD

Retold by Ian Strachan
Illustrated by Victor Ambrus

Kingfisher

KINGFISHER
An imprint of Larousse plc
Elsley House, 24-30 Great Titchfield Street
London W1P 7AD

First published by Kingfisher 1997
1 2 3 4 5 6 7 8 9 10

Text copyright © Ian Strachan 1997
Illustrations copyright © Victor Ambrus 1997
Decorative borders copyright © Vanessa Card 1997

A CIP catalogue record for this book
is available from the British Library

ISBN 0 7534 0001 4

Printed in Hong Kong
Designed by Dalia Hartman

Contents

Prologue

PORTENTS OF DOOM

Long, long ago, in the days when the lives of men and gods mingled and Zeus, the great King of the gods, reigned on Mount Olympus, the lives of thousands of people were affected by the fates of just two men.

They were born far apart, on either side of the Aegean Sea: Achilles, who was Greek, and Paris, who was Trojan. But even before these two men were born, dark warnings hung over their futures . . .

Among the guests at the wedding of Achilles' parents (King Peleus and the sea-goddess Thetis) were three women, all dressed in white. Known as the Three Fates, they were renowned for their ability to foresee the future.

The first told the newly-wed couple, "You will have a son and call him Achilles. He will be greatly admired for this looks, strength and courage."

The second announced, "Your son will be fleet of foot, strong of arm and none will defeat him on the battlefield."

Finally, the third Fate said, "He alone will decide the destiny of the city of Troy – and only a Trojan arrow can kill him."

Mindful of this warning, when Achilles was born his mother, Thetis, held her baby by his heel and immersed him in the River Styx to protect him from the dangers which might lie ahead. The gods assured her that this would protect her son from any mortal arrow.

Later, as a young boy, Achilles was sent with his greatest friend, Patroclus, to be educated by the wise centaur (half-man, half-horse) whose name was Chiron. It was on his back that Achilles learned to ride. Chiron also taught the boys how to fight, to hunt for food and to use herbs to heal wounds, as well as to recite verses and play tunes on the lute.

But all the time, as Thetis watched her son grow big and strong, she worried about the third Fate's prediction for him. For she realized Achilles

5

would soon outgrow his boyish pursuits, put on real armour and mount a chariot of war.

Around the time of Achilles' birth, across the sea in the city of Troy, King Priam's wife, Queen Hecuba, was about to give birth to Paris, when she experienced a horrifying dream.

In it, as Hecuba bent over her newborn son, the baby turned into a flaming torch from which leapt countless fiery serpents. In no time the palace was ablaze and the flames quickly spread, until finally the whole of Troy was destroyed.

As a result of the dream, as soon as Paris was born, the King and Queen cast their son out into the wilderness, believing that he would die.

But the gods decided otherwise and arranged for a shepherd to find the baby and raise him. And so it was that Paris survived to grow into a healthy and exceptionally handsome young man.

The Golden Apple

But what eventually set nation against nation, man against man, and stirred up passions which divided even the gods and goddesses on Mount Olympus, was a jealous quarrel over a golden apple. The quarrel began at the wedding of Achilles' parents, King Peleus and Thetis, at the same time as the Three Fates were making their predictions for Achilles.

Gods, goddesses and mortals had come from far and wide to celebrate the marriage, but there was also one unwelcome guest. Eris had not been invited because she was such a spiteful goddess, who caused trouble wherever she went. When she arrived to find Zeus' wife, Hera, his daughter, Athena, and also the young goddess of love and beauty, Aphrodite, walking happily arm in arm, Eris was determined to cause mischief.

From under her robes she produced a beautifully sculpted golden apple, which had engraved upon it the words, "For the fairest". She rolled it to the feet of the three goddesses, who immediately began to squabble jealously over which of them deserved it most. They demanded that the other guests should decide.

But everyone knew that to choose any one of them would only attract the revenge of the others and so the apple was given to Zeus for safe-keeping.

Years later, Zeus grew weary of the prolonged and bitter dispute between the three goddesses which was disturbing the peace of Mount Olympus. He sent Hermes to Paris, who was by now a fine young man, with the golden apple and a message saying that Paris should settle the argument by deciding who should have it.

When Hera, Athena and Aphrodite arrived, before Paris made up his mind, each tried to tempt him into giving them the treasured apple, by bribing him with promises.

"If you give it to me," the powerful Hera said, "I will shower you with wealth and you shall rule over every country in the world."

Athena, the pampered, pretty daughter of Zeus said, "I would make you famous and the bravest hero ever."

But the lovely Aphrodite brushed them both aside. "Give the apple to me, Paris, and I will offer you a gift far more precious than wealth, or the glory of war. I will give you the most beautiful wife in the whole world: Helen, the Queen of Sparta, daughter of Zeus."

As the three goddesses anxiously awaited his decision, Paris carefully looked at each one again before finally handing the golden apple to Aphrodite, declaring, "You are by far the most beautiful."

It was a choice which earned him the never-ending love and devotion of Aphrodite but, equally, the everlasting hatred of Hera and Athena. In the years to come, their anger would cause much heartbreak, costing many men and women their lives.

The year after Paris made his fateful choice, King Priam announced that a series of games was to be held in Troy. On hearing of the event, Paris decided to enter. He did not realize they were being organized by his own parents, who by then believed their son was long since dead.

Paris won many bouts in the various contests and even overwhelmed men whom he did not recognize as his own brothers. The strongest of these was Hector.

As the games reached their climax, King Priam was about to announce the overall winner, when his daughter, Cassandra, who was gifted with second-sight, amazed everyone by saying, "Father, I think we should offer a drink to the gods, to thank them for returning your lost son."

Amidst their rejoicing, as they welcomed Paris home, everyone forgot the awful warning his mother had received in her terrible dream.

GATHERING CLOUDS OF WAR

One night Aphrodite, remembering the promise she had made to Paris, appeared beside his bed and said to him, "The time has come for you to go to Greece. There, in the city of Sparta, at the court of Menelaus, you will find the wondrous Helen and I will ensure you win her heart."

By this time Helen, ignorant of Aphrodite's promise to Paris, had married the respected Greek warrior, red-haired King Menelaus, and they had a baby daughter, Hermione.

Unaware of the purpose of his visit, Menelaus welcomed Paris to his palace and, in his honour, bid the servants prepare the Great Hall for a celebratory banquet. The hall was a truly wonderful place, built of stone and adorned with golden ornaments and beautiful wall-paintings. However, during the feast Paris had eyes only for Helen, who was seated next to him.

Although he noticed her slender figure, the fine bones of her face and

the lustrous, black hair which tumbled to her shoulders, it was Helen's eyes which captivated him. A darker green than emeralds, they burned with an intense beauty and inner passion which struck Paris to the heart. He knew then, he must make her his own.

The moment they were alone, Paris declared his love to Helen. To his surprise, Helen was deeply offended by his outburst and scolded him, "How dare you say such things to me, when I am already married to Menelaus?"

However, during the next few days Paris persisted and eventually, with Aphrodite's help, on a day when Menelaus was away from the palace, Paris persuaded Helen to say farewell to her baby daughter and to sail home with him to Troy.

When Menelaus returned to find that Paris had betrayed him by running away with his wife, he was furious. He quickly persuaded a dozen leaders from the surrounding Greek kingdoms and islands to bring their forces and help him to wreak revenge on Paris and the Trojans.

Amongst them, Idomeneus came from the island of Crete, Odysseus led the Ithakans and Diomedes brought the Argive army.

They arrived in long, narrow, wooden ships. Though sometimes helped by a single linen sail, they were more usually powered by up to a hundred and seventy oarsmen. Soldiers manned the oars in relays, sitting in three tiers on either side of the ship. Built on huge oak keels, at the waterline each ship had a massive bronze barb jutting from its bows, for ramming and sinking enemy warships. Eyes were painted high on their prows, intended to ward off evil spirits and help the boats find their way safely to their destinations.

The massive fleet of over a thousand ships which gathered in a bay on the eastern coast of Greece made a magnificent sight.

King Agamemnon, Menelaus' elder brother, was the most experienced general, and so the army of a hundred thousand soldiers was placed under his overall command.

But from this great armada one man's ships were missing – those of Achilles. Everyone knew he had become a great warrior and they remembered the Fates' prophesy that only Achilles could destroy Troy. They were deeply unhappy to discover that he was not going with them.

THE WARRIOR ACHILLES

When Achilles' mother heard that the entire Greek army was gathering to pursue Helen to Troy and recapture her, fearing for Achilles' life if he went with them, she had spirited him off to a remote island.

But Agamemnon sent the persuasive Odysseus to seek out Achilles and urge him to join them.

When Odysseus eventually found Achilles, he taunted him, "Surely you don't want to stay here idling your time away, while all the other Greeks go and fight the Trojans?"

It was the thought of being called a coward which finally persuaded Achilles he must go with them, but first he visited his ageing father, King Peleus, to explain his decision. "Though my mother wanted to protect me from the danger which awaits me in Troy, I have already proved myself in many battles. Besides, what use is a long life, if it is spent in disgrace for not being with my fellow warriors?"

Saddened though he was to think that he might never see his son again, Peleus presented Achilles with the magnificent armour which Zeus had given him at his wedding, and the two immortal horses, Balius and Xanthus, presented to him by the god of the sea, Poseidon. King Peleus also asked Patroclus, Achilles' lifelong friend, to go with him and try to protect Achilles from harm.

And so Achilles, bringing with him forty black ships full of brave Myrmidon warriors, joined the fleet.

Immediately before they set out for Troy, the commanders gathered and, to encourage the gods to look favourably on their mission, prepared a burnt offering.

As the smoke rose from their fire, a blood-red snake suddenly appeared from beneath the altar. Hissing, it swiftly coiled itself around a tree, where it swallowed nine sparrows which had been perched together on a branch. Agamemnon asked his soothsayer, Calchas, to explain.

"The nine birds eaten by the snake show the nine long years you must fight the Trojans. Only in the tenth year will the city be destroyed and your enemies overthrown."

On hearing these words, many of the Greeks were disheartened, but not Agamemnon. "Nobody can change what the gods have said," he declared, "but if we are going to have to fight for nine years before we succeed, the sooner we set off the better!"

The Siege Begins

After a difficult, wind-ravaged voyage, the vast Greek fleet finally arrived on a desolate coast some distance from the walled city of Troy. Amongst the rocky reefs, they found a sandy bay where they could draw their ships up out of the water, stern first, to protect them from storms. Around the boats they built a huge camp of tents made from animal hides and turf.

When the Trojans saw so many enemy ships landing on their shore, they immediately retreated inside the high walls of their city and as the Greeks had neither the weapons nor the experience to attack a walled city, they had no choice but to lay siege and wait.

During the nine long years which passed, there were a number of short, cruel battles, when the Greeks ambushed Trojans who had been forced to leave their city in search of supplies, but these decided nothing. The Greeks

could not avenge their honour by reclaiming Helen and the Trojans remained trapped inside the walls of their city.

The long waiting game meant that Greek supplies ran low and soldiers made regular forays into the neighbouring countryside, taking by force whatever they wanted.

After one such expedition, led by Achilles in the tenth year of the siege, they returned from Lymessos with not only sheep and goats for food, but also a number of women prisoners. Among them were two beautiful women, Chryseis and Briseis. Achilles had grown particularly fond of Briseis and decided to keep her, but he generously handed Chryseis over to Agamemnon.

Chryseis was the daughter of an ageing priest in the temple of Apollo, Chryses. He followed Achilles' troops back to the Greek camp, bringing servants who staggered under the weight of priceless treasures, and sought out King Agamemnon. "May the gods allow you to plunder Troy and return home safely, but accept the treasures I have brought as ransom," he pleaded, "and give me back my precious daughter Chryseis."

Hearing his pitiful entreaty, many of the Greeks urged Agamemnon to agree, but the proud king rudely rejected the old man. "I will not give up the girl. Chryseis stays with me and I'll hear no more about it."

Although Chryses wept and grovelled in the dust, Agamemnon sent him away, threatening the old man with death and dishonour if he should ever dare return to repeat his request.

Terrified and heartbroken, Chryses hurried away but as he did, in his anguish he beseeched the god Apollo to wreak a mighty vengeance on Agamemnon for the wrong which had been done.

Apollo, hearing the cry of his faithful priest, strode down from Mount Olympus and rained disease and pestilence upon the Greek camp.

The Anger of Achilles

All along the beach, beside the Greek warships, hundreds of menacing plumes of black smoke rose, forming clouds large enough to blot out the sun.

Soldiers watched anxiously as the funeral pyres consumed the bodies of their dead comrades. Their gaunt faces lit by the dancing flames, they stood in silence, wondering which of them would be next to fall victim to the terrible plague which had rained down on them for nine whole days and nights.

At first it had struck down their dogs and horses, but it quickly began to attack men, creeping amongst them like a dark shadow. Sentries dropped dead at their posts without warning, while others died in their sleep and, as soon as the following day, their swollen corpses gave off a dreadful stench.

The Greeks had already endured nine years of separation from their homes and families, camped out on foreign soil while they laid siege to Troy. Now, instead of facing victory, or at least being allowed to die with honour in battle, they were being struck down by a mysterious, loathsome disease.

On the tenth day of the dreadful epidemic, Achilles summoned everyone to a great meeting and, speaking for all, said to King Agamemnon, "If war and plague are joining forces against us, I fear our campaign is lost. Ask your holy man why these ills have befallen us."

Calchas, the seer, stood up. "I fear the god Apollo has attacked us because of the way King Agamemnon insulted his priest Chryses. When the old man brought a ransom and begged you to free Chryseis, his daughter, you sent him away, heartbroken, with harsh threats ringing in his ears. Not until we send the girl back to the arms of her loving father, together with a hundred sacred bulls to be sacrificed in honour of Apollo, shall we be able to calm the god's fury with us."

Agamemnon rose to his feet, his eyes blazing with anger. "Seer of misery! I kept the girl because I want her. However, if it will rescue my people from this present disaster, I will part with her – but only if she is replaced by something better."

Achilles, outraged, sprang to his feet. "We have no spare treasure lying around. Everything we've gathered has been divided fairly between us all. Surely you don't expect us to give it back? That would be a disgrace."

"Hold, Achilles!" Agamemnon quickly replied. "Why should you be allowed to cling to your prize, while I hand over mine and end up empty-handed? I am the commander and I will confiscate a gift from you. I will take Briseis, the girl you kept for yourself. Put Chryseis aboard one of my ships and you, Achilles, shall take her back and appease the gods."

Achilles could not believe what he was hearing. "I have never heard such greed! The Trojans have done me no harm. I only came with you for the sake of you and your brother, Menelaus, to win back his honour. But what do you care? Now you threaten to strip me of a prize I won with my own hand. It's always the same. My arms bear the brunt of the fighting but, whatever we win, when it comes to dividing up the spoils, you take the lion's share and I am left with scraps. I'd sooner take to my ships and go home than stay here to be disgraced by you whilst you pile up your riches."

"Go if you will! Desert us!" retorted Agamemnon. "I won't beg you to stay. Others will take my side and do me honour. What if you are a great soldier? That's just a gift from the gods. Take your comrades and your

ships, but hear this: I will still take Briseis from you, if only to teach you that I am more powerful than you."

Achilles was so furious his hand strayed towards the silver hilt of his sword. Should he kill Agamemnon now, or curb his anger? Instead, he attacked the King with bitter words. "You coward! Never once have you armed yourself and gone to battle with the rest of us, because you lack the courage. You prefer to stride around the camp taking our prizes. But this I swear, soon you will be in desperate need of me. When hordes of your men are being cut down at the hands of Hector, you will bitterly regret this day when you insulted me."

Hearing the hostile exchanges between the two men, Nestor, the oldest of the chieftains and leader of the Pylians, rose to calm them. "Stop now, before enormous sorrow comes to us all. How King Priam and all the Trojans would rejoice if they could hear you two quarrelling. Agamemnon, powerful as you are, do not seize Briseis. And you, Achilles, strong as you are, you cannot hope to win a battle with your king. I beg you both, cool your tempers."

16

But King Agamemnon brushed Nestor's plea aside. "Achilles wants to lord it over me. A brilliant spearman he may be, but that doesn't give him the right to hurl abuse at me."

Achilles snapped back, "Fling your orders at others, not at me, for I will no longer obey them. Take the girl, I give her to you freely. But I warn you now, if you, or any other man, should try to take anything else from me against my will, you will see your own blood surging out around my spear!"

With that they both strode out of the meeting.

Agamemnon immediately had one of his smaller ships hauled down to the sea, chose twenty of his finest oarsmen to man her and sent Chryseis on her journey home, together with a hundred bulls.

The ship had hardly left the shore before Agamemnon told two of his men to go to Achilles' camp, with orders to collect Briseis. "And if Achilles does not give her up willingly, then I will take an army and seize Briseis myself."

The two men found Achilles angry and upset, sitting outside his tent, but were too afraid to approach him until Achilles urged them closer. "You are not to blame," he assured them. "Agamemnon is the one who sent you here. But if the day should ever dawn when the armies need me, remember my loss." He turned to his friend Patroclus. "Go and fetch Briseis, so that they may take her back."

Patroclus did as he was bid and Briseis was handed over. She left reluctantly and Achilles averted his gaze as they led her away, past the long line of ships, back to Agamemnon's camp.

Achilles wandered miserably alone down to the shore, nursing his injured pride. There he wept tears of anger and distress, as he prayed to his mother, the sea-goddess Thetis. "You, who gave me life, short as it might be, should also give me honour, but you allowed Agamemnon to disgrace me and seize my prize."

Hearing her son, Thetis rose up from the depths of the sea. "What ails you, my child?"

"Can't you see what that man has done to me?" Achilles protested. "Go to Olympus and plead with Zeus to let the might of the Trojans force the Greek army to retreat, until it is pinned back against its own ships. Only then will the stubborn Agamemnon realize how mad he was to disgrace me in front of everyone."

"Oh, my son!" Thetis wailed. "Would that you could stay here without a grief in the world. Doomed to a short life, you have so little time. I will do as you ask and go to Zeus. Perhaps he will be persuaded."

Leaving Achilles to his gloomy thoughts, Thetis rose up from the white foam of a cresting wave and soared up to Mount Olympus to plead with Zeus.

But her entreaty filled Zeus with unease. "How can I do what you ask? If I do, Hera, my wife, will believe I am siding with the Trojans, and hate me for it."

Indeed Hera, who had been eavesdropping, could hardly contain her anger. She and Athena, still smarting after all these years from the hurt of seeing Paris award the golden apple to Aphrodite, protested, "How can you allow the Trojans to slaughter hordes of Greeks, just to spare Achilles' feelings?"

Trapped between the arguments of Thetis and Hera, Zeus tugged at his beard, furious with them. "Leave these matters to me, or I will make you both pay. Remember, you are powerless against me."

Hera and Athena fell silent, but that night Zeus lay awake for hours, trying to find a way of helping Achilles without upsetting the goddesses. Eventually, Zeus hit on a treacherous scheme. He whispered his idea to a Dream and then sent the Dream off to Agamemnon.

The Treacherous Dream

The Dream flew off swiftly, passing silently amongst the shadows of the ships, seeking out Agamemnon. It found the king asleep in his tent.

Hovering by Agamemnon's head, the Dream called out, "How can you sleep at a time like this? I bring you a message from Zeus, who bids you rise up! Attack the Trojans at once and you will succeed in crushing them. Forget not my words as you wake!" And so saying, the Dream faded away into the shades of night.

The instant Agamemnon woke, he leapt up and pulled on a new, soft linen tunic. Over it, he strapped his battle armour of gleaming bronze; a breastplate and a pair of greaves to protect his legs. Across his shoulders, Agamemnon slung his battle cloak, a shield and a sword in a silver-studded sheath.

Striding out into the pale light of dawn, Agamemnon commanded heralds to summon the entire army. When they had gathered, he addressed them. "Go, ready yourselves for battle! Sharpen your spears! Feed your horses well and prepare your chariots."

Taking aside the main chieftains of the armies, Nestor, King Idomeneus, Great Ajax, Diomedes, Odysseus and Menelaus, Agamemnon gathered them round him in a circle. In the centre, Agamemnon sacrificed a fat ox, raising his voice in prayer. "Great Lord Zeus, who lives in the bright sky, don't let the sun set until I have torched the gates of Troy, smashed down the halls of Priam, ripped the tunic from Hector and slashed his chest to ribbons!"

Then Agamemnon ordered the heralds to sound the advance. Before the last echoes of the trumpets had died away, a great cheer rang out from the ranks. In turn, this was soon drowned by the thunder of feet and hooves as the vast army, its chieftains proudly leading in their chariots, set out for Troy.

19

The Trojans Prepare for Battle

The Trojan sentries in their outposts caught sight of a great cloud of dust rising upon the far side of the wide plain below the city. Then they heard the ominous drumming of hooves and, as the cloud grew closer, the Trojans were able to make out the Greek leaders, charging towards them in their war chariots, the rays of the sun glinting off the bronze armour like advancing wildfire.

A sentry hastily set off for the city, where he breathlessly reported to Hector and King Priam. "Your Majesty, I've never seen such an army! There are so many of them, they look like hordes of autumn leaves being blown towards us. We believe they intend to storm the city gates."

Hector went down to the main gates without delay and ordered them to be opened. Out poured Trojan chariots and hundreds of men on foot who lined up in rows, prepared to defend their city against the Greeks.

While they were still some distance apart, the two armies halted. As the dust began to settle, Paris, a leopard skin slung over one shoulder, a bow on the other, a battle-sword at his hip and gripping two bronze-tipped spears, sprang forward.

When Menelaus spotted the man who had stolen his wife and caused this war, he leapt fully armed from his war chariot and roared, "Now for my revenge!"

But seeing Menelaus coming towards him, Paris slipped back into the ranks.

Hector called after him, "So my brother, you who were brave enough to carry off his wife and brought a curse down on our city, can't stand up to Menelaus?" Bitterly, Hector added, "What cowards the men of Troy are! Years ago they would have stoned you to death for the trouble you have brought down upon us."

Much to Hector's surprise, Paris admitted his failing. "You criticize me fairly! If you really want me to fight to the finish here, bid the Greeks and

Trojans take their seats and pit me alone against Menelaus. Let us two fight it out and whoever proves the better man shall take Helen as his prize. That way, our people can be allowed to live in peace and the Greeks return to their homes."

Hector stepped forth and cried out, "Hear me! Lay down your armour and let Paris and Menelaus take the field in single combat. Whoever proves the better man wins, and leads the woman home."

A hush came over both sides, until Menelaus replied, "Knowing what casualties we have all suffered over my quarrel with Paris, I agree. It is right that we two should be the ones to fight to the death. Let us swear to these words, and our truce, in blood!"

As all the chariots were drawn up into line, the soldiers of both armies laid down their arms and sat on the ground opposite each other.

A bowl of wine and two lambs were brought into the centre and, having washed his hands, King Agamemnon prayed. "Father Zeus! Be witness here to our binding pact. If Paris brings down Menelaus, he keeps Helen and we sail for home without her. But, if the red-haired Menelaus overcomes Paris, she comes with us." Then he drew his bronze sword across the lambs' throats, letting their blood splatter on the ground. Agamemnon covered the blood with wine from the

bowl, adding, "Whichever contender breaks this treaty first, may their brains be spilled on the ground as I spill this wine!"

During the ceremony, a messenger ran to find Helen. "Come quickly and see what's happening. Moments ago, the Greeks and Trojans were longing to kill each other. Now the fighting's stopped. The warriors on both sides have thrust their lances in the ground and sit beside them. Paris and Menelaus are going to fight over you and whoever wins will call you his wife!"

Helen, her green eyes brimming with tears, ran up towards the city walls. As she passed, some of the citizens whispered about her beauty, "No wonder the Greeks and our men have suffered years of agony over her."

Seeing Helen coming along the ramparts, which overlooked the battleground, King Priam called to her, "Come here by me, dear child, so that you may see Menelaus, your husband of long ago, and all your own people."

Helen whispered, "I couldn't love and respect you more if you had been my own father. But how much better it would have been if we had never met and I had died that day, instead of forsaking my husband and child, to come here with your son Paris."

King Priam shook his head. "I do not blame you for what has happened, I blame the gods. They are the ones who brought this war upon us all."

Paris Faces Menelaus

On the battleground, which had been carefully marked out, the two warriors were being prepared.

Paris wore greaves, fastened behind his ankles with silver clasps. Over his strong shoulders were slung a silver-hilted sword and the strap which supported his sturdy shield, made from bullocks' hides and covered in bronze. Onto his head went a well-forged helmet from which bristled a horsehair crest. Finally, Paris took up his spear.

Menelaus, similarly equipped, fearlessly strode out to meet his enemy.

To determine who should have the first strike, Hector dropped two carefully marked stones inside his upturned helmet. As Hector shook his helmet the stones clattered round but it was Paris' stone which jumped out first.

The two warriors, cheered on by their supporters, grimly marched away from each other to take up their positions for the duel.

As Paris and Menelaus menacingly brandished their spears, the crowd grew silent. Then there was a gasp as Paris suddenly hurled his spear. It flew straight at Menelaus but when it hit his strong round shield, the spear's point was bent back and rendered harmless.

In his turn, Menelaus took careful aim before hurling his spear at Paris. It hit the centre of Paris' shield with such force it not only pierced that but the breastplate behind it too. Luckily, there was just time for Paris to swerve aside and the spear's point only scratched his chest.

But by the time Paris had recovered from the blow, Menelaus had already drawn his sword and was charging towards him. Raising the sword high above his head, Menelaus brought it crashing down on the ridge of Paris' helmet. But, to Menelaus' dismay, the blade shattered into jagged fragments.

Seething with anger and frustration, Menelaus grabbed hold of the horsehair crest on Paris' helmet and, using all his strength, began swinging

Paris around by it. The braided leather chin strap bit deeply into Paris' throat and would have choked him to death if Aphrodite had not intervened.

Her invisible hand snapped the strap, so that the helmet came away, empty, in Menelaus' hands. Furious, Menelaus snatched up his spear again but, by the time he had turned to launch a fresh attack on Paris, he found himself blundering through a thick mist. Aphrodite had created a fog to enable her to spirit Paris away to safety.

Treachery

Athena, who had seen how Aphrodite had cheated Menelaus of certain victory, was anxious to spur the Greeks back into action. She swept down from Mount Olympus, seeking out the famous Trojan archer, Pandarus.

She whispered temptingly in his ear, "Pandarus, have you the courage to fire an arrow at Menelaus? Think how grateful all your countrymen would be, especially Paris, to see Menelaus lying dead on the ground."

Without a thought for the consequences, Pandarus unstrapped his bow, made from the polished horns of a wild goat. He flipped open his quiver, took out a newly feathered arrow and notched it on to the string. Then Pandarus, using his enormous strength, drew back the string until the bow was bent into a half-moon. Taking very careful aim, he released the string and the razor-sharp, bronze-tipped arrow sped off.

But Athena, who flew faster than any arrow, reached Menelaus first. She deflected the arrow's path so that, instead of killing Menelaus, it merely pierced his breastplate and wounded him, as had always been her intention.

Athena's trick worked. Seeing the dark blood trickling down Menelaus' thighs, King Agamemnon angrily cried out, "The truce I sealed in blood has proved to be your death warrant."

Though in pain, Menelaus, trying to calm his brother, replied, "It is not a mortal wound, my armour bore the brunt of the shot."

"I pray you're right," Agamemnon murmured, "but Machaon, the healer, shall treat it immediately and soothe your pain."

While Machaon removed the arrow, sucked out the blood and applied herbal ointments, Agamemnon declared to the other warlords who had gathered, "See how the men of Troy have laid my brother low, trampling over our solemn, binding truce. Priam and all his people must die! Vultures shall eat their still warm flesh."

Hearing the cries for blood going up from the Greek army, the Trojans quickly retrieved their weapons and prepared for battle.

Agamemnon moved quickly through the Greek ranks, issuing words of encouragement. "Never relax your nerve, your fighting strength!" And he rebuked any soldiers he saw retreating. "Have you no shame, standing there dazed? Do you want the Trojans to chase you back to the sea? What are you waiting for?"

When he came across the leader of the force from the island of Crete, King Idomeneus, Agamemnon saluted him and said, "You above all our fighters I prize."

"Count on me!" Idomeneus assured him.

Further along the line, Nestor barked orders to the charioteers at the front of his troops. "No heroics now! But let no man give ground, lest the charge break down! Any charioteer who reaches the Trojan ranks, don't throw your spears but thrust at the enemy. That way you will still have them for another lunge."

The sturdy Diomedes strode, fully armed, towards the Trojan ranks, calling to his men, "Up now, wake your fighting-rage!"

And so the Greek battalions surged forward, wave upon wave of them, like breakers piling after each other in a race towards the rocks.

The two armies met with a clash of shields loud enough to shake the earth. Pike scraped against pike. Swords clashed with armour. And above the din could be heard the shouts of triumph and cries of pain, as men fought and some died, their blood streaming across the ground.

Antilochus, one of Nestor's sons, was first to kill a Trojan captain, spearing him just below the horsehair ridge of his helmet, so that the bronze point smashed through his forehead and sent him reeling to the ground. As a Trojan bent to aid his fallen companion, he lowered his shield. Antilochus, seeing the unprotected flesh, thrust with his sword and left two corpses lying across each other.

The giant Ajax, with his first charge, wounded another Trojan leader, by sending a spear straight through his enemy's shoulder.

One of Priam's sons, Antiphus, seeing what Ajax had done to his countryman, hurled his spear at Ajax, but missed, hitting instead one of Odysseus' generals.

Enraged by his comrades' death, Odysseus pushed through the ranks and hurled his spear. The bronze point pierced Antiphus' head from side to side and down he crashed, his armour clanking against his lifeless body.

Seeing the mighty Odysseus advancing towards them, the Trojans hesitated and began to shrink back. The Greeks used this slight advantage to recover the bodies and weapons of their dead and wounded, piling them into chariots which sped back to the camp.

But the god Apollo did not want the fighting to end

this way. Seeing the Trojans shrinking from their task, he called down to them, "Never give up! The Greeks are not made of iron or rock! The powerful Achilles is not even with them. So, stab them, slash their flesh!"

And Athena similarly encouraged the Greek soldiers not to pause but to drive home the advantage they had won.

Inspired by Athena's words, Diomedes drove his chariot to the centre of the fighting. Hardly had he reined in his horses and leapt to the ground when a spear, hurled at him by one of two Trojan brothers, Phegus, flashed past his shoulder. Diomedes returned in kind and caught Phegus full in the chest, throwing him to the ground. Phegus' brother, Ideaus, hauled him into their chariot and turned their horses for the city.

Seeing the two brothers, one dead and one retreating, several other Trojans also turned their back on the fighting. One among them, Odius, was spotted by Agamemnon, who launched a spear after the retreating warrior. Its point punched through Odius' back and out through his ribs, sending him crashing to the ground.

Further down the line, Idomeneus' javelin caught the Trojan warrior Phaestus at the very moment he was climbing into his chariot. It pierced Phaestus and left him hanging over the front of his chariot, mortally wounded, as his startled horses panicked and sped off unchecked.

Diomedes Fights the Gods

But one man amongst the Greeks, Diomedes, had been so inspired by Athena's words, he continued to rampage through the Trojan ranks. Once, his spear sliced up through a Trojan's throat, passed through the jaw and cut away the man's tongue. Next, with a single mighty blow of his sword, Diomedes removed the massive bulk of another man's arm.

The archer, Pandarus, the one who had been tricked by Athena into breaking the truce and re-starting this battle, saw the mayhem Diomedes was causing. Training his bow on the Greek warrior, he fired. His arrow winged across the field and struck Diomedes on the right shoulder, shearing its way through the armour, leaving it splattered with blood.

"See," Pandarus cried in triumph, "I shot him."

But the arrow failed to bring Diomedes down. Despite great pain, he managed to reach his chariot, where he called to his driver, Sthenelus, "Get down and pull out this wretched arrow."

As Sthenelus set about removing the arrow, Diomedes prayed aloud. "Athena, daughter of Zeus, stand by me. Let me see the man who has wounded me, so that I may thrust my spear deep into his flesh!"

Athena, hearing his plea, urged Diomedes on. "Fight it out with the Trojans, but see, I have lifted the mist from your eyes. Now you will be able to tell a man from a god. But don't take on the immortals head-on. Only if you see Aphrodite, she's the one you must punish with your spear."

Encouraged and ignoring the pain of his wound, Diomedes hurled himself back into the fray with renewed vigour, bringing down Trojan after Trojan. While he was stabbing one man with his lance, he removed the head of another with his sword.

The noble Trojan Aeneas, seeing what damage Diomedes was doing, tracked down Pandarus. "Where's your famous bow? There's a man out there who is butchering some of our finest troops. Only you can stop him."

When Pandarus looked where Aeneas was pointing, he was astonished.

"I know that man – he is Diomedes! Just now I caught him in the shoulder with an arrow and thought him dead."

"As you can see, far from being dead, he's slaughtering our men. Climb into my chariot," Aeneas urged, "so that this time we can get up close and make sure. Here, you take the reins."

"No," Pandarus replied, "they're your horses and they'll work better for you than for a stranger. But get me very close, so that I can take Diomedes on with a sharp spear. I've winged him, it won't take much for me to finish him."

Aeneas whipped his horses and the chariot charged forth. As they drew close, Pandarus yelled to Diomedes, "So, my winged arrow failed to bring you down? Let's see if this can kill you!"

With all his strength, Pandarus heaved his spear. It struck Diomedes' shield, drilling through it to the breastplate, but there it stopped, failing to inflict a wound.

Diomedes quickly recovered from the impact and launched his javelin. Athena added her hand to it, driving it even faster, so that it split the face of Pandarus and sent him crashing from the chariot.

Aeneas, fearing the Greeks might drag away Pandarus' corpse, leapt down to protect it. But while he was bending over the body, Aeneas turned to find Diomedes coming straight for him carrying above his head a huge rock plucked from the battlefield. Issuing a bloodcurdling cry, Diomedes hurled the jagged rock. It struck Aeneas on the thigh and, as the shattered leg crumpled beneath him, he fell.

Diomedes would have finished Aeneas off if Aphrodite had not rescued him. Hoping to carry him away to safety, she flung her shining robe around Aeneas to hide him.

Incensed, Diomedes pursued Aphrodite through the plunging, fighting men and, when he caught up with her, thrust at her with his spear, gouging her hand.

She cried out in pain and dropped Aeneas.

"Let that be a lesson to you!" Diomedes shouted to her. "Next time, maybe you'll think twice before interfering in a battle."

But even then, Diomedes could not find Aeneas. Apollo, seeing what had befallen Aphrodite, had concealed Aeneas in a dark cloud and was preparing to carry him away, when he said to her, "You're injured, leave the battlefield. I'll look after Aeneas, while you return to Olympus."

The moment Aphrodite arrived on Olympus, she showed everyone her wound, wailing, "Diomedes did this to me! The Greeks are not only waging war upon the Trojans; now they're taking on immortals too."

Hera and Athena were secretly delighted that Aphrodite had been taught a lesson. "You started all this," Hera pointed out, "by encouraging Paris to make off with Helen. In the circumstances, you're lucky to get away with a mere scratch on the hand."

But Zeus intervened. "Aphrodite, why are you meddling in the war? Battles are the concern of Athena and your brother, Ares."

"Ares is already down there," Athena said. "Look! He's disguised himself as Acamas and is fighting alongside the Trojans."

Hera was incensed. "I thought Ares was supposed to be siding with the Greeks?"

"He was," agreed Athena, "but he's changed sides. The trouble with Ares is, he enjoys causing trouble and confusion."

"And see," Hera added, "Apollo has used his healing power on Aeneas."

As they watched, the savage fighting began again, the two sides mauling each other like packs of wolves, until ranks of fighters from both sides lay side by side, sprawled face down in the dust. But now it was the Greeks who were beginning to tire.

"This has got to stop," Hera complained to Athena. "We can't let Ares cause any more havoc."

"Come with me," Athena said.

They went to the stables, where they harnessed two horses to Athena's heavy chariot. Made from gold and silver, its wheels had bronze spokes and silver hubs. Athena donned her armour and golden helmet, which was fronted with twin horns and engraved all round with pictures of fighting men.

As Athena boarded the chariot, Hera whipped the horses and they sped out through the gates of Olympus and downwards, until they came to Diomedes' chariot.

It was resting beside the Scamander river, where Diomedes was using cool water to wipe the blood from the wound Pandarus had inflicted on him.

Athena was amazed. "What are you doing here? Why have you stopped fighting? Surely you're not frightened? You know I can help you."

Seeing Athena, Diomedes replied, "I'm not frightened and I know you're on our side. I'm holding back because Ares has disguised himself as Acamas and now he is fighting for the Trojans."

Athena scoffed, "He loves trouble for its own sake. Take up your reins and return to the battlefield with me."

As they galloped towards the battle front, Athena donned her helmet of Death, which rendered her invisible, even to Ares. But Ares could still see Diomedes and threw his spear at him. However, the invisible Athena caught the spear's shaft and threw it off course, so that it missed Diomedes.

"Now's your chance!" Athena hissed.

Diomedes raised his spear and sent it flashing through the air. It caught Ares in the thigh and a thousand men could not have managed such a loud cry of pain as he let out!

Every man on the battlefield, Trojan and Greek alike, paused and shuddered in horror at the sound. They looked on in amazement as Ares first shrouded himself from head to foot in a cloud of black smoke. The smoke rose up into a column, which whirled higher and higher like an enormous cyclone, as it carried Ares back up to Olympus.

As he arrived in front of Zeus, who was sitting on his golden throne, Ares complained bitterly, "Did you see what happened? A mere mortal dared to attack me, one of the immortals! I detect the hand of Athena behind this. Why do you allow her to do such things?"

"Don't come whimpering and complaining to me!" Zeus said, waving Ares' objections aside. "You like nothing more than to start a quarrel, but you don't like it when you suffer as much as they do. Go, have your wound attended to."

As Zeus turned back to look down on the plain of Troy, he saw that Hera and Athena were also flying back up to Olympus, but the Trojans were being forced back towards their own walls.

Hector Returns to Troy

Hearing rumours of the massive Greek counter-attack, a crowd of Trojan women, hoping for more realistic news of the battle, had gathered in front of King Priam's palace.

When they saw Hector coming through the gates, they were shocked. His once glittering chariot was smeared with the grime of the battlefield and even the horses' hides had been gashed by Greek weapons. Hector's armour was stained with blood, his brow beaded with sweat. Only his helmet and spear shone brightly.

Hecuba, his mother, rushed down the palace steps towards him, very distressed. "My brave son, if you have left the battlefield, dreadful things will surely befall us. I'll have wine brought. You must offer some to Zeus, but refresh yourself with the rest."

But Hector refused. "No, mother. Can't you see the state I'm in – smeared with blood and dust? I can't possibly make a respectful offering to the gods like this. But you take all these women to the temple of Athena and make an offering to her. Pray to her for pity, while I go in search of Paris. Maybe I can persuade him to rejoin us. After all, he is the cause of all this!"

Hector found Paris inside the palace with Helen. While she explained the pattern she wanted to some women who were weaving, Paris was busy admiring his own reflection in his shield, which he had spent some time cleaning and polishing to perfection.

The sight sent Hector into a rage. "How can you sit here like this?" he demanded. "Out there, our men are being mercilessly slaughtered and our women are frightened beyond endurance, while you sit polishing your shield! You brought us to this. Don't you care about the fate of Troy?"

Paris and Helen looked startled by Hector's anger.

"Of course I do," Paris replied. "I only came back ahead of you to decide what to do next. Helen has been urging me to return to the battle and I've been getting ready. I'll put on my armour. Go ahead, I'll catch up with you."

Hector didn't reply. Instead he stared at Helen. She hid her face in her hands and moaned, "Oh, Hector, I wish I had never been born. How could I have brought such misery and suffering on everyone? But don't take it out on Paris. You won't change him, which is why I am so worried about what will happen to him." She looked at Hector and patted the seat beside her. "Come and rest by me, Hector, you look worn out."

Hector firmly shook his head. "This is no time for rest. They expect me back on the field but, before I go, I must see Andromache and Scamandrius. Who knows when, or if, I will ever see my wife and son again. Do you know where they are?"

Helen shook her head.

Hector, having searched the palace for his wife without success, was about to leave the city, when he saw Andromache. Carrying their son in her arms, she was running down the steps from the gate-tower. Tears streaming down her cheeks, Andromache rushed towards Hector and let him hold her close. "I heard the Greeks were attacking," she explained, "and went to see for myself. I had to know you were still safe and that your courage had not proved to be your own destruction! Why not stay here now, inside the walls, and guard the city?"

But Hector reluctantly shook his head. "I cannot. I would die of shame if I shrank from the battle. Don't worry about me. No man will hurl me down to death ahead of my fate, which no man, brave or cowardly, can escape. Take our son home and leave the fighting to the men. After all, fighting's what the men of Troy were born for, and I most of all."

Kissing his wife and child a reluctant goodbye, Hector leapt into his chariot and left the city. Not far behind followed his brother, Paris, radiant in his glinting armour.

An Honourable Duel

When Hector and Paris launched themselves back into battle, killing Greeks on either side of them, Athena, watching from Mount Olympus, wanted to intervene, but Apollo stopped her.

"What do you intend to do now?" he demanded. "Will you turn the tide of battle yet again and not stop until Troy is reduced to a pile of rubble? How many of your brave Greeks will die in the attempt? My plan is better. Let us call a halt to the carnage."

"And how do you propose to do that?" Athena asked.

"I'll spur Hector's courage," Apollo replied, "and get him to challenge one of the Greeks to fight him man to man – a duel in bloody combat to the death."

Athena agreed and, when he'd heard Apollo's suggestion, so did Hector. He strode on to a hilltop and, holding his spear above his head to attract their attention, called to his men to hold back.

As the fighting died down, Apollo and Athena flew together up into the sky and then soared down again, like birds of prey, until they settled in the top of a huge tree, hunched like vultures, waiting to see the outcome.

"Hear me," Hector called out. "Our oaths, our sworn truce, have all come to nothing and, as a result, we are faced with death on both sides. To finally decide matters between us, I challenge any Greek who feels brave enough to face me in mortal combat. Which of you will take on Prince Hector?"

Immediately, nine Greek warriors stepped forward. Each scratched his initial on a stone. The stones were placed in a helmet and shaken hard, until the first one sprang out.

"Thank Zeus!" Great Ajax cried. "The stone is mine and it fills my heart with joy, for I know I can overpower Hector."

Ajax strapped on his burnished armour, collected his weapons and took up his vast body shield, made from seven thick oxhides and finished with a layer of heavy bronze. A towering figure of a man, with a grim smile beneath his dark, craggy brow, he strode out to meet Hector.

When Hector saw the massive man he was to fight, his heart began to beat a little faster, but he knew there was no way out. He had issued the challenge and it would bring shame on himself, and all Trojans, if he did not keep his word.

"Hector," Ajax said, "you are about to find out what kind of men we Greeks are. Come, lead off!"

The rays of the evening sun flashed off Hector's helmet as he shook his head in defiance. "Ajax, don't toy with me as if I were a weak-kneed boy! I am experienced in the butchery of war and I know how to fight to the finish. Big as you are, I've no desire to strike on the sly. Strike now!" Hector hurled his spear.

It struck the centre of Ajax's shield so forcefully, it pierced the metal and six of the skins, but stopped at the seventh layer of oxhide.

With a great roar, Ajax heaved his spear. Although Hector swerved, it went straight through his shield, but the point glanced off his breastplate and only grazed his thigh.

As the sun began to set, sending the sky blood red, the two attacked each other like wild animals. Hector thrust, but the

point of his lance was bent back by the strength of Ajax's shield. When Ajax lunged, blood spurted from Hector's scratched neck, but he did not back away. Instead, Hector stooped, picked up a dark, jagged stone and hurled it at Ajax with all the force he could manage.

The stone hit the huge shield with a massive clang which echoed round the battlefield, but rolled harmlessly away. Enraged, Great Ajax picked up a huge rock, big as a millstone, and with tremendous force, his muscles bulging, heaved the missile at Hector.

As it struck him, Hector's knees buckled and he was thrown on his back, the shield which had saved him from worse injury pressed against his chest.

Scrambling to his feet, Hector drew his silver-studded sword and the two set about each other; dark shadows in the gathering twilight, hacking and drawing blood.

But, though they fought long and hard, neither was able to inflict a mortal wound and finally two men, one a Trojan, the other Greek, stepped forward and separated the two warriors with their wooden staffs, urging them to abandon the duel before it became too dark to see.

Great Ajax growled, "Tell Hector to call the truce! He issued the challenge, let him be the first to call it off."

Hector nodded, "Very well, Ajax, let us break off this duel. No doubt we'll fight again tomorrow, until some fatal power decides between our two great armies. For now, we must yield to the night. But before we leave, let us exchange gifts, so that men may say, 'They both fought bitterly, but parted bound by pacts of friendship'." Hector handed over his sheathed, silver-studded sword and, in return, Ajax gave Hector his war-belt.

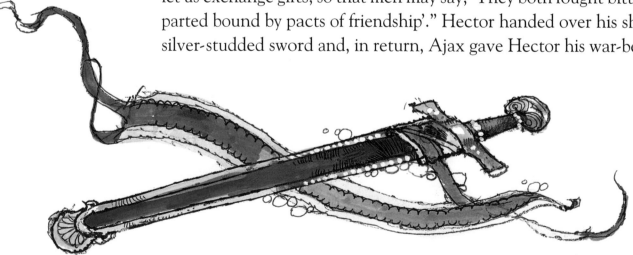

Plotting and Planning

As Hector led the Trojan troops back to the city, the Greeks, weary from the day's battles, set up their camp with the aid of lanterns. Soon the sentries, standing guard on Troy's walls, looked out across the dark plain and saw the red glow of hundreds of campfires.

The Greek leaders, when they had washed off the grime of battle, gathered in King Agamemnon's tent. A banquet had been prepared in Ajax's honour and when it was served, Agamemnon made certain Ajax was given the very best cuts of meat from the specially slaughtered ox.

After they had taken their fill and were relaxing, Nestor spoke some sombre thoughts which were on his mind. "King Agamemnon, though thankfully we ourselves are still here to celebrate, today we lost too many brave men. At dawn you must call a halt to the fighting, while we gather up the bodies of our dead. Then we can burn them, keeping the fires at a safe distance from our wooden-hulled ships, and gather up their bones so that they may eventually be taken home with us."

Everyone nodded in agreement, but Nestor had not finished.

"If the funeral fires were built in one long line, after they have cooled and the bones been retrieved, we could heap soil over the ashes from the landward side which would leave a deep ditch. That way, we would throw up ramparts to protect ourselves. From time to time, in the wall, we could erect gateways for our chariots, whilst the ditch would hamper the Trojans if they decided to attack us."

Everyone agreed that this was an excellent plan and, so that it would be blessed, poured more wine but took none for themselves until they had spilled some as an offering to the gods.

In Troy, discontent was growing and at a gathering in the main square, Antenor spoke for many, when he told King Priam, "I think we should give Helen and all her treasures back to the Greeks. We broke the truce. We fight as outlaws. And what do we stand to gain? Nothing at all, in my opinion."

There were loud murmurs of assent, but then the magnificent, fair-haired Paris jumped to his feet. "I tell you straight out, I will never give up Helen. But as to the treasure she brought with her, I'm willing to return it all and add more from my stores, if the Greeks will go home and leave us in peace."

King Priam, who was aware of the growing mood of protest amongst the people and had listened carefully to what had been said on both sides, spoke out. "All of you, go home, bathe and eat. Then tomorrow, at first light, let my trusted herald, Idaeus, go to Agamemnon and put to him the proposal Paris has just made. Let him also ask if they are willing to halt the war, until we can burn the bodies of our dead."

As dawn broke, Idaeus left the city under a flag of truce. He sought out Agamemnon and his chiefs and put the proposals before them, adding, "But Paris makes it clear, he will never willingly return Helen, though there are many in Troy who wish he would!"

Diomedes was the first to reply. "Let no man touch the treasures of Paris, or Helen either. It's obvious, from what this man says, the Trojans are on their last legs, staring defeat in the face!"

There was a roar of assent from the other leaders as

Agamemnon turned to Idaeus. "There's your reply, we'll have none of it, until we defeat you and take everything we want! But, as far as the dead are concerned, gather them up by all means. I'd never grudge their burning, may the fires soothe them quickly."

The sun was rising in the sky when the two armies met again on the battlefield. But this time there was no noise, or clamour, as they went silently through the fallen, each side identifying their dead. It was a difficult and unpleasant task. Clotted blood and soil were frequently washed away to reveal the face of a dead comrade, and bitter tears were shed.

Eventually, both sides left the field and lit their funeral fires: the Trojans outside the city walls, the Greeks clear of the ships.

The following morning, before daybreak, the Greeks followed Nestor's plan and, having removed the bones of their comrades, began to pile up soil, supported by baulks of timber, along the line of funeral pyres.

Through the heat of the midday sun they laboured until, by evening, there was a deep ditch with wooden stakes driven in to it, to prevent the Trojan chariots crossing. Behind, was a high wall with several gateways through it. As night began to fall, the Greeks fell on to their straw mattresses, exhausted.

The Tide of Battle Turns

The following morning Zeus summoned all the gods and issued a stern lecture. "I want to bring this violent business to an end and any god or goddess I catch aiding either Trojans or Greeks will return here, whipped by my lightning, eternally disgraced. Do I make myself clear?"

Zeus stalked off, leaving them all stunned into silence. He harnessed his bronze-hooved horses to his chariot and, with a crack of his whip, flew down to earth, the horses' golden manes streaming behind them. He came to rest on a hill beside the plain, from where he could see the walls of Troy and the Greek encampment with its new wall.

He had hardly arrived before both armies seized their weapons and surged towards one another. Soon their battle shields clashed together and the earth once more rocked with the thunder of struggle. Screams of agony and triumph rent the air, as man slaughtered man until the ground streamed with fresh blood.

Zeus watched patiently until midday, but then could take no more. Suddenly there was a huge crash of thunder and he sent down several brilliant bolts of lightning, aimed directly at the Greeks.

The men were terrified. Many, including Agamemnon, Idomeneus, Great and Little Ajax, withdrew in their chariots. Only Nestor remained, though not from choice. One of his horses had been winged by an arrow from Paris. It had hit the horse in the forelock, causing it to rear in agony and sending the rest of the team into panic.

While Nestor was busy hacking through the leather traces to free the wounded horse, Hector started to charge down on him, determined to finish the old warrior off.

Diomedes, seeing what was afoot, sped to the rescue. "Nestor, free your horses and drive them at the enemy while I hold them at bay with my spear."

Grasping his horses' reins, Nestor hastily climbed aboard Diomedes' chariot. He whipped the team before releasing them to charge at Hector.

As they did, Diomedes threw his spear at Hector and, though he missed, he picked off Hector's driver.

Diomedes was ready for the kill and would have finished Hector there and then, if Zeus had not released another mighty thunderbolt. A blazing white flash of lightning hit the ground right by the hooves of Diomedes' team, sending them shying and rearing in the air.

"Turn your horses!" Nestor yelled. "Can't you see? Zeus is handing victory to Hector. No man can fight the gods, not even one as brave as you."

Diomedes, having regained control of his horses, reluctantly turned their heads for the Greek camp, pursued by the arrows and spears of Hector.

Three times Diomedes tried to turn and drive Hector and his men back, but each time Zeus deterred him, by loosing more thunderbolts.

Hector yelled to his men, "Summon your battle fury! At last Zeus is granting me glory and triumph. Ignore their foolish ditch, my team will cross it in a single bound. Soon we'll be slaughtering the Greeks, setting their ships on fire and victory will be ours!"

Defeat for the Greeks?

Behind the Greek rampart, the shore was packed tight with men and chariots, all milling around each other, panic running through them as the Trojans pressed closer and closer.

Agamemnon, faced with the prospect of defeat, struggled to rally his men. Diomedes responded by charging through one of the gates in his chariot and killing a Trojan captain. Menelaus followed in his wake, valiantly fighting to keep the Trojans at bay.

On top of the wall, Great Ajax used his massive shield to guard the archer, Teucer. Each time Ajax raised his shield, Teucer took aim at his target and fired an arrow. Ajax then lowered the shield to protect Teucer from return fire. Eight arrows Teucer released this way and each found its mark in an enemy soldier.

But when Teucer got Hector in his sights, he failed to hit him, catching his driver instead, knocking him from the chariot and causing the horses to rear up, neighing and pawing the air in alarm.

Hector, spying the Greek archer up on the wall, leaped out from the plunging chariot, grabbed a rock and hurled it. Teucer was still drawing back his bowstring when the stone hit him in the neck. The surprise blow made him overdraw the bow, snapping the bowstring, which left his wrist numbed by a searing pain.

Soon Hector and his men were mopping up the last Greek stragglers they could find, though by then most had managed to retreat across the trench and find some way of scrambling back behind the high wall.

Only nightfall rescued the Greeks from total defeat. Disappointed though Hector was not to have had time to rout the Greeks, he was delighted to have scored such an important victory against his enemies. As the Trojans withdrew, to enable them to make camp at a safe distance, Hector proclaimed, "My friends, send word to Troy of our triumph and also tell them, we attack again tomorrow at daybreak!"

A Plea to Achilles

When the Greek generals managed to struggle through the milling troops, they found a distraught Agamemnon. "Zeus has betrayed us," he wailed. "Having promised I would never leave for home until I had brought down the walls of Troy, now he commands I leave in disgrace, whole regiments of my men destroyed in battle."

The seasoned warrior, Nestor, was unwilling to admit defeat. "All is not yet lost. Sentries must take up their posts and squads of men be sent to guard the trench we dug outside the rampart."

Orders were given and men despatched. The poor wretches sat huddled over their watch fires as they cooked their evening meal, peering out into the darkness in case raiding Trojans crept up on them.

But Nestor did not let matters rest there. Other thoughts had been preying on his mind and he could hold them back no longer. "This all started that day, great King, when you infuriated Achilles and took the girl Briseis from his tent. Against our advice, you gave way to your anger and disgraced him before us all, by seizing his prize. And you keep her still."

Agamemnon, his brow furrowed with worry, nodded. "That's no lie, old man. I was blinded by pride."

"But if ever there were a time when we needed the great Achilles," Nestor pointed out, "his men and his famed fighting skills, it is now."

"The man alone is worth an entire army," Agamemnon admitted.

"Then why not see," Nestor suggested, "if Achilles can be won round with gifts of friendship and warm words?"

Agamemnon agreed. "I am bent on setting things right. Before you all, I'll name the splendid gifts I will offer him: seven cooking tripods, untouched by fire, with twenty burnished cauldrons to go on them. Ten bars of gold and a dozen of my swiftest stallions. But, above all these, I will return Briseis, the girl I took away from him. And, when we return home, he shall have the pick of my three daughters and become my son-in-law. I'll add a

dowry too, the like of which no man has ever offered with his daughter! Seven citadels will I give Achilles. All this I offer, if only he will relent. Just let him submit to me. I am the greater king, the elder born and, I claim, the greater man."

Nestor was delighted by the offer. "Generous Agamemnon! No one could fail to be impressed by the treasure-trove you're offering Achilles. Let Ajax and Odysseus go to him in haste and try to bring him round, while we pray he'll show us mercy."

They immediately set off along the dark shoreline for Achilles' camp, desperately hoping they would be able to persuade him to re-join the battle.

As they reached the dark shadow of his ships, they found Achilles sitting outside his tent with Patroclus. Achilles sprang up when he recognized the men who were approaching. "Look who's come our way," he said to his friend. "I must be sorely needed now! Set food and wine before our guests."

Patroclus stirred up the embers of the fire and joints of lamb, goat and pork were soon laid out on the table, together with wicker baskets of fresh bread and generous quantities of wine.

While they ate, Odysseus raised his cup of wine to Achilles. "Your health! But though we can banquet to our heart's content, that is not why we came. Stark disaster stares the Greeks in the face, Achilles. All hangs in the balance: whether we save our ships, or they are destroyed. The Trojans have pitched camp right by our ramparts. At dawn, Hector threatens to gut our ships with fire and kill our comrades while they're pinned up against the burning hulls. But while all this happens you, Achilles, who were promised victory against Troy, hold yourself in check. Let the anger which consumes you go, friendship is better and the King will hand you gifts to match his insults, if only you will relent."

Ajax named all the gifts Agamemnon was offering and added, "If later the gods allow us to plunder Troy, Agamemnon promises, when we enter the city and share the spoils, you shall load the holds of your ships with as much gold and bronze as you desire."

Odysseus laid out the challenge. "All this he wants to give you, if only you'll end your quarrel. And even if your hatred of Agamemnon is too great, at least take pity on all our men who will be mauled in battle. If you do return, they will honour you! Think of the glory you'll earn in their eyes, when you meet Hector head on and kill him."

But Achilles was not impressed. The bitterness still gnawed away inside him. "I hate that man like the Gates of Death!" Achilles declared. "Agamemnon says one thing, whilst hiding another in his heart. Since we came here, I've sacked cities by land and sea, while he hung about, skulking behind the lines. I've dragged back piles of plunder and always handed it over to him. He'd parcel out some scraps to others but keep the lion's share. Some he handed to the lords and kings and they keep them still. But from me he snatched Briseis!"

"We know all this," Ajax muttered, "but can't you let it be?"

Ignoring him, Achilles suddenly asked, "Why are we here? We came for the beautiful Helen. Do Agamemnon and Menelaus think they are the only men who love their wives? Any decent man loves his own, cares for her. Though I won Briseis as a trophy with my spear, I loved that woman with all my heart. But Agamemnon robbed me, tore up my honour with his hands. He'll never win me over now. And, as I've no desire to battle with the glorious Hector, I'll launch my ships and head for home."

Odysseus was appalled by what he heard. "Sail for home? Is that all that concerns you? Have you forgotten how, in the past, we've fought side by side? Has the spirit inside you been completely overpowered by this anger? It's wrong to show such an iron, ruthless heart. If Agamemnon were not holding out such gifts, if he was still swaggering, I'd be the first to agree with you, but he has sent us to implore you to return."

Ajax, tiring of the argument, said firmly, "Though nobody could blame your anger before, don't dismiss us now. Come and fight, then our men will honour you like a god."

But Achilles was adamant. "What puzzles me is, why do you insist on currying favour with a man like Agamemnon? It demeans you."

Hearing this, Great Ajax rose, a towering figure, and said to Odysseus, "Come, there'll be no achieving our mission here! Let's go back and make a full report, depressing as it is. It seems the gods have planted a relentless fury in your chest, Achilles. All for a girl, just one, when Agamemnon is offering you a treasure-trove. Achilles, put some kindness in your heart. Here we are, under your roof, anxious to be your friends."

Achilles answered warmly, "Well said. But I will not consider arming for war again, even if Hector batters his way through to the Greek ships and shelters, slaughtering the men and gutting the hulls with fire. However, if Hector comes to my own ships or camp, then he will be stopped dead in his tracks!"

When Achilles had finished, they all raised their cups, poured wine out to the gods, and Ajax and Odysseus set off, past the long line of ships, to Agamemnon's tent.

"Come, tell me," Agamemnon demanded, "will Achilles fight? Or does he refuse – does rage still grip his proud spirit?"

Odysseus replied, "Achilles has no intention of quenching his anger. He spurns you and all your gifts, says you must work out your own defence and threatens, at first light, to sail for home."

For a long time they all sat in silence, their hopes dashed.

It was Diomedes who finally broke the gloom. "If only you hadn't begged Achilles, holding out mound upon mound of gifts. He's a proud man, who will not be bought, and now you've only plunged him deeper into his pride. I say, have done with him, whether he sails home or not! He'll come round and fight again when he's ready. But for now, let us sleep until first light. Then you must defend our ships by mustering our chariots and battalions in front of them and spur the men on by fighting yourself, up in the front rank."

Thieves in the Night

But the turmoil in Agamemnon's mind stopped him getting to sleep. He could not stop himself picturing the campfires burning just beyond the ditch and the thousands of Trojan soldiers sitting round them, waiting to invade the Greek camp at daylight.

When he could take no more, Agamemnon got up, drew on his battle-shirt and threw a lionskin over his shoulders. He intended to visit Nestor, hoping the old man might help him work out a plan to ward off the disaster facing them but, as Agamemnon took up his spear, Menelaus arrived, a tigerskin slung across his broad back. "Why take up arms now, brother?"

"We need some sort of plan," Agamemnon said, "to shield our men and ships from the vengeance of the Trojans and their allies. Go, wake Ajax and Idomeneus quickly. I'll get Nestor, Diomedes and Odysseus."

When they had all gathered in Agamemnon's tent, Nestor spoke. "If someone could cross the ditch and get into the enemy camp without being noticed, they might be able to pick up some hint or whisper of exactly what Hector intends to do tomorrow."

Diomedes leapt to his feet. "I'll do it! Though we would see more and be more sure of bringing back the knowledge safely if two men went."

Agamemnon spoke out, "Then choose your own companion."

Without hesitation, Diomedes replied, "There can be no better man to go with me on such a mission than Odysseus."

The two quickly armed themselves and together they passed the flickering fires of their own sentries before creeping out into the darkness of the no-man's-land which lay between the two armies.

Thick cloud hid the moon. To avoid making any noise, which would alert the Trojan sentries, the two men had to pick their way carefully through the remains of the previous day's fighting. The ground was littered with weapons, bits of armour and dead bodies.

• • •

Meanwhile, over in the Trojan camp, Hector was also holding a council of war. "We need to know more about exactly how the Greek ships are being guarded. If any man is willing to go, I promise him, when we have overthrown the Greeks, he shall have the two best horses in the entire Greek camp."

Dolon, who was greedy, though none too bright, said, "If you swear those two horses will be the ones which pull Achilles' chariot, I will go. For such horses as those, I'll get right into Agamemnon's tent and bring you back all their plans."

Hector agreed and no sooner was Dolon armed than he was off, leaving the comfort of the Trojan campfires behind him.

But Diomedes, whose eyes had grown more accustomed to the dark than Dolon's, saw the shadow of the man coming towards them. He put a hand on Odysseus' arm and whispered, "Who is this leaving the Trojan camp?"

"Until he's passed us," Odysseus suggested, "we'll crouch down amongst the dead. That way, if he makes a dash for it, he won't be able to return to his own camp and betray us. Then we'll take him, alive if possible, so we can question him."

The two knelt down among the corpses but, as soon as Dolon had

stumbled past, they quietly got to their feet and sped after him.

Hearing footsteps pursuing him, Dolon started to run, but Odysseus, who was close behind, called out, "Stop, or my spear will run you through."

But the threat made Dolon run all the faster.

Odysseus hurled his spear and though, as was his intention, it missed the man, it buried itself in the ground beside him, the shaft still quivering. Dolon stopped dead in his tracks and immediately began pleading for his life. "I'll pay my own ransom. I've a house full of bronze, gold and iron. You can have it all, if only you'll spare my life."

"Be quiet!" Odysseus ordered as he gripped the man by the shoulders. "Death is the least of your problems right now. What were you doing out here? Have you come to rob the dead?"

Diomedes grabbed the man's hair and pulled back his head. "Or were you going to spy on the Greek camp?" he demanded.

Dolon, his teeth chattering with fear, stuttered, "It was all Hector's idea! He promised me Achilles' horses and his magnificent chariot too, if I would go and find out how well the Greek ships are being guarded."

Odysseus found it hard to hide his amusement. "For a coward you set your heart on heroic gifts! Remember Achilles' mother is immortal and mortal men struggle to control those horses!"

"Is it true what they say – that one of Achilles' horses can talk?" Dolon stammered.

"Right now, you are the one who's going to talk!" Diomedes said grimly. He drew his sword and placed the sharp point against Dolon's throat. "Tell us, where did you leave Hector? How are the Trojan guards posted? Is Hector intending that all your troops shall stay out here, or will some head back to Troy?"

"I'll tell you everything," Dolon jabbered and he answered all Diomedes' questions. "But, if you want to invade our camp, I suggest you aim for the regiment from Thrace, which has just joined us. They are led by King Rhesus and his are the best horses I've ever seen. They're certainly the biggest, whiter than snow, and faster than the wind. They're easy to find, out on the eastern side of our camp. Now, I've told you everything I know, please take me back to your ships while I arrange the ransom."

"And run the risk of you escaping," Diomedes scoffed, "and reporting back to your leader? I think not!" And, with a single mighty blow of his double-edged sword, Diomedes removed Dolon's head from his shoulders.

Following Dolon's directions, Diomedes and Odysseus carefully picked their way through the dead bodies, seeking the Thracian camp. They arrived to find all the troops fast asleep, exhausted from the long journey to join Hector, their weapons piled beside them on the ground.

Only the pairs of battle horses, tied up like great, white ghosts beside each man, noticed the Greeks' arrival. As they scented intruders, they whinnied softly, nervously pawing the ground with their great white-feathered hooves.

"Diomedes," Odysseus hissed, "you take care of the men, while I look after the horses."

Like a lion attacking an unguarded flock of sheep, Diomedes launched himself upon the men. He fell on them so quickly, he hacked through the throats of twelve men with nothing escaping from them but a dying groan and their own blood, which formed dark pools on the ground beside them. Then he took the life of the thirteenth man, King Rhesus himself.

While Diomedes was occupied in slaughter, Odysseus had gathered the reins of the horses from their hitching posts. Soon he had them all, apart from the king's pair, in one plunging, snorting team. Cracking the whip above their heads, Odysseus released them, aiming them for the main part of the Trojan camp, where their stampeding hooves could cause the most havoc.

As the cries of alarm went up, Odysseus hitched the remaining two horses to the king's chariot, which was finished in gold and silver. He leapt aboard and brought the sturdy horses round. Having collected the bloodstained Diomedes, they raced headlong back to the Greek camp, where they were welcomed with astonished admiration.

The Day it Rained Blood

At first light, Agamemnon strapped on his magnificent battle gear.

His breastplate was spanned by ten bands of blue enamel, spaced by twelve of gold and twenty of beaten tin, the whole decorated with six dark blue serpents which writhed and shimmered upwards towards his throat. He slung his silver-sheathed sword, with gold studs at its hilt, across his shoulder and finally took up two spears and his shield. The shield was made from layers of oxhide, strengthened by circles of tin and bronze. At its centre was a boss of blue steel, formed in the grim, threatening shape of the Gorgon's head.

As Agamemnon strode out of his tent and called his men to arms, Zeus sent a tremor through their ranks, by sending down upon them a vast, soaking shower of blood-red rain.

Wave upon wave of Trojans swept towards the Greeks and the fighting was grim and bitter, men falling in droves on either side.

But as the day grew older, Agamemnon's determined resistance developed into attack and the Greeks slowly began to break through the Trojan lines.

First, Agamemnon encountered the veteran captain, Bienor, ramming his spear so hard through the rim of one man's bronze helmet as to splatter his brains inside it.

Then he came across Isus and Antiphus, riding in a single chariot. Achilles had caught these two once before, whilst foraging in the hills beyond Troy but on that occasion, having taken their sheep, he had spared their lives. This time, they were not so lucky. Agamemnon speared Isus in the chest and with his sword, hacked Antiphus across the face, sending him sprawling from his chariot, before leaving them for dead.

Where Agamemnon pressed forward, his infantry followed, engaging in hand to hand fighting, where bronze flashed and thrust in the immense slaughter.

Yard by yard, the Trojan army was driven back, until they found themselves outside their own city gates. There, both armies paused, waiting to see which would make the first move.

During the lull in the fighting, Zeus sent Iris, one of his messengers, to Hector. She told him, "The father has sent me to tell you that as long as Agamemnon thrives on the battlefield, defend yourselves, but hold back. As soon as a spear or bow's shot wounds the king and he mounts his chariot, Zeus will hand you the power to kill and kill, until you reach their ships."

Having delivered the message, Iris sped away, leaving Hector to organize the defence of Troy's gates.

Amongst them was Iphidamas, a tough son of Antenor. He saw Agamemnon coming towards him and hurled his spear, aiming for the king's waist, below the breastplate. But he miss-aimed, and the point of his spear broke as it struck bronze.

In return, Agamemnon closed on Iphidamas, hacked his neck with his sword and dropped him to the ground. Coon, seeing his brother slaughtered, retaliated and caught Agamemnon under the elbow, slashing his forearm. The pain caused Agamemnon to shudder to a halt but, while Coon was bending down, trying to drag away his dead brother, the king recovered enough to behead Coon, leaving the two lying on the ground together.

But Agamemnon realized that
the pain of his wound and loss of blood was making
him grow weaker. He slowly hauled himself into his
chariot and, telling his driver to make for the ships, he cried
to the men, "Your turn now! Make sure you keep them from
our ships!"

Hector, seeing the driver crack his whip and the team rush off
with the injured warlord, recognized the signal Zeus had promised.

"See, their best man cuts and runs!" Hector called to his troops.
"Drive your horses forward. Seize this moment of triumph!"

The Trojans surged forward and, despite anything the Greeks could
do, slowly, bloodily, they began to win back the ground they had lost.

Even so, they still did not have things all their own way. Diomedes brought
down Agastrophus, but it was while he was busy stripping the body of its
armour that Paris, with his bow, got Diomedes in his sights. Clenching his
grip and drawing back the string, he sent the arrow whizzing straight into
Diomedes' foot. The shaft dug through, pinning Diomedes to the ground.

Paris leapt from his hiding place with a cry of triumph, "Now you're hit, though I wish it had been in the guts, so that it had ripped your life away."

Never flinching, Diomedes replied, "You're brave enough with your bow and arrow, you with the glistening locks and roving eye! Come and try me in hand to hand combat."

Odysseus, who was fighting close by, rushed forward to shield Diomedes and give him time to get down on one knee and tug out the barbed arrow.

Racked with pain, Diomedes struggled into his chariot and the driver headed for their camp, leaving Odysseus alone. As waves of Trojan fighters came towards him, Odysseus fought with heart and soul to beat them off.

He cut down Thoon, Ennomus and then caught Chersidamas under his shield with a spear which slit the man from crotch to navel and left him writhing in agony on the ground.

But when Odysseus skewered Charops with his spear, Socus, Charops' brother, stood firm, declaring, "Odysseus, wild for fame, glutton for war, breathe your last!"

Socus, using his spear, stabbed Odysseus' shield, went through the shield and the breastplate, and sliced the flesh from Odysseus' ribs. Drawing back, with the spear still wedged through his armour, Odysseus hurled abuse at Socus. "Maybe you've stopped me fighting for now, but you'll pay for what you've done."

Socus turned to escape but, as he did, Odysseus threw his spear. The point pierced Socus' unprotected back, came out through his chest and breastplate, throwing him to the ground.

But as Odysseus pulled Socus' spear from him, blood came gushing forth. Seeing how badly Odysseus was wounded, the Trojans prepared for a final attack which would finish him off.

Above the roar of battle, Odysseus cried out for help. Hearing the cry, Menelaus and Ajax went to the rescue. They found him surrounded by Trojan soldiers, as vultures gather round a stricken animal. Swiftly cutting their way through the crowd, Ajax eventually planted his shield beside Odysseus to protect him. He and Menelaus managed to keep the Trojans at bay until a chariot could be brought to carry Odysseus to safety, before they threw themselves back into the battle.

With so many of his comrades wounded, Ajax reluctantly realized he had to retreat, but he only went back as far the ramparts they had thrown up. There, fighting between the Trojan and Greek lines, Ajax made a stand. Spears pierced his massive shield and stuck halfway, but still he stood against them.

Behind the ramparts, Achilles, hearing the clash of metal on metal, climbed up on the stern of his ship. The battle was getting much closer and a line of wounded men were being brought back.

"Patroclus," Achilles said, "I think they'll need me soon. Agamemnon will come begging on his knees. Their need for me will grow too much to bear." Thinking he saw a familiar figure amongst the many wounded, Achilles instructed Patroclus, "Go, question Nestor, ask who is that wounded man he brings back. From this distance, it looks like Machaon, the healer. Go!"

Patroclus did as he was asked, going at a run along the line of ships until he reached Nestor's camp, where he found the old man refreshing himself with wine, while others bathed Machaon's wounds.

Seeing Patroclus, Nestor invited him in. "Sit and take wine with me."

But Patroclus shook his head. "No time to sit. Achilles wants to know who was injured, but I can see now, it's Machaon, just as he thought."

Nestor was puzzled. "Why is Achilles so interested in one wounded man, when so many of our champions have been laid up in the ships? Diomedes brought down by an archer, Odysseus and Agamemnon both speared. But Achilles, brave as he is, why should he care? How much longer will he wait – until our ships are in flames and we have all been mown down?" An idea dawned in Nestor's mind. "At least, if Achilles still won't come, perhaps you could persuade him to let you fight in his famous armour. That way the Trojans might mistake you for him and hold off the attack while we regroup to fight again."

Patroclus, excited by Nestor's suggestion, was running back to tell Achilles, when he came across Eurypylus, limping away from the battle, an arrow planted in his thigh. Seeing the sweat pouring from the man's brow and the still bleeding wound, Patroclus burst out, "How tragic you look! But tell me, can the Greeks still hold out against Hector? Or must we all die?"

Struggling against the pain of his wound, Eurypylus replied, "We've no hope left! Now that our most seasoned campaigners have been brought down by Trojan hands, the rest will soon be hurled back against their ships. Please, help me! When you were young you learnt about medicines from Chiron, the centaur. Take this arrow from my leg and spread on some soothing ointment."

Patroclus lifted the stricken man in his arms and carried him back to his shelter, where he laid him down on a pile of oxhides. Kneeling beside him, and using a sharp knife, Patroclus cut the arrow from Eurypylus' thigh and washed the wound with warm water. From his pouch, Patroclus took a piece of a herb's root, crushed it in the palms of his strong hands and gently smeared it over the wound. Immediately the pain was gone and the bleeding stopped.

His job done, Patroclus got to his feet. "Now I must go and tell Achilles about a plan of Nestor's. A plan which just might save us all."

Hector Storms the Ramparts

Hector was urging his charioteers to cross the wide ditch below the Greek ramparts. But, though the stallions charged forward eagerly enough, they suddenly baulked when they reached the edge, whinnying in fear and tossing their manes. Even if the Greeks had not driven in sharpened timber stakes to protect the ditch, the horses would still have been unable to leap it in a single bound.

Polydamas came alongside Hector. "It's madness to try and get our teams across there. Even if we succeeded in getting past the stakes, we'd be up against the rampart, with no room to dismount, let alone fight."

"What now then?" demanded Hector.

"I suggest we dismount and attack on foot."

Hector saw the sense of Polydamas' plan and immediately gave orders. "Rein your teams by the trench, we advance on foot."

Under their commanders, five battalions obeyed and, wedged shield to shield, charged into the trench in a single wave, yelling their lungs out. The Greeks manned the rampart and, plucking rocks from it, hurled them down at the invaders.

The missiles rained down on Trojan helmets and shields, like violent hail in a thunderstorm, but even so while some were already scaling the rampart, more continued to advance.

The Greeks could see it was only a matter of time before they would be overwhelmed and the cry went up, "Form into a semi-circle on the shore and defend the ships!"

Hector, anxious to torch the ships, was about to cross the rampart when he glanced up and saw an ominous sign. An eagle was flying above him, clutching a snake between its talons. The snake, which was still alive and struggling, suddenly reared up and struck its captor several times in its tawny breast. Agonised by the pain from the poisonous bite, the eagle instantly loosed its prey which fell, dead, amongst the horrified soldiers.

Polydamas spoke the thoughts of many, when he said to Hector, "After what we've seen, I think we should call off the attack. We may well get through to the ships, but all the signs are that we will be driven back. Though the snake struck the eagle, it had lost its own life by the time it hit the ground."

Hector turned on him with a dark glance. "Enough! Bird signs indeed! Fight for your country. Onward!" he shouted, leading the charge forward, and his army swarmed after him with blood-curdling cries.

At that moment, Zeus, who was watching from Mount Ida, released a great wind which whipped up a sandstorm along the beach, blinding the Greeks.

On the other side of the rampart, where the air remained clear, the Trojans busied themselves with the earthworks, tearing down the towers, pulling at the battlements and prying loose the stakes.

When the Greeks realized what was happening they tried to fill the breaches in the trench with shields and anything else which came to hand – so desperate were they to stop the bloodthirsty Trojans getting through. Both Ajaxes, Great and Little, stood on top of the wall, urging the men to even greater efforts to protect themselves. Between them crouched the archer Teucer.

As stones continued to beat down upon the Trojan forces, one man, the brawny Glaucus, holding his shield above him for protection, headed for the gates, intending to prise them open with an iron bar. Others quickly followed and they all began to heave, until the massive posts supporting the gates began to rock.

Great Ajax, seeing the gates would soon fall, shouted to Teucer above the deafening cry of battle, "They must be stopped. Fire your piercing arrows at them."

Teucer's first arrow stabbed Glaucus. In reply Glaucus sent a spear into the stomach of a Greek soldier. Gripping the shaft of the spear, the dying man plunged forward off the wall and rolled down into the wide trench.

Suddenly, Hector seized one of the huge rocks which had been rolled down on them by the Greeks, lifted it high in the air and smashed it against the gates which blocked his path. Both gates thundered with the blow, planking shattered, hinges broke and he was through!

Others poured through after Hector, like an undammed torrent, forcing the Greeks back to their ships, with no escape.

Battling for the Ships

The great sea-god Poseidon, hearing the commotion on the beach, rose up from the deep and saw the difficulty the Greeks were having, as they tried to protect their vessels. Some were busier tending their wounds than defending their ships; others had given up all hope and were sitting on the beach, their heads in their hands.

Poseidon, who nursed a long-standing grudge against the Trojans, had no wish to see them succeed now. Ignoring his brother Zeus' warning not to interfere, Poseidon disguised himself as Calchas, Agamemnon's prophet, and made his way amongst the Greek troops.

He talked first to the dejected Ajax, saying, "You're surely not thinking of giving up? All is not lost in one skirmish. Have patience, persist, the Trojans will eventually grow weary."

Having spoken, Poseidon touched him with his magical sceptre. Ajax was puzzled by the immense strength and energy he suddenly felt pouring through him and surprised when the man he thought was Calchas vanished from sight.

Poseidon next appeared amongst a group of battle-weary soldiers who had lost their weapons and with them all hope of survival. "I thought you were defending your ships," he said, "but here you sit, waiting for Hector to come and finish you off. Look at Ajax, he hasn't given up hope. Go, join him. If you have the will, Ajax has weapons for brave men."

As if by magic, the men jumped up and raced off to join Ajax, while Poseidon found Idomeneus, who was carrying a wounded man back to his ship.

"Idomeneus!" Poseidon roared. "Why are you turning your back on the fighting? Only cowards leave. Your comrade can look after himself. Stand up to the Trojans again. You won't be alone. As soon as they see you return to the fray, others will follow your lead."

Immediately Idomeneus, brandishing two spears in his fist, returned to the battle, which was growing more furious, with no mercy shown on either side.

As the Greek counter-attack began to take its toll on the Trojans, Hector sought out Polydamas. "Where is my brother Helenus?"

"Back in Troy," Polydamas informed him, "having his wounds treated, alongside many others. I did warn you that the eagle we saw was a bad omen and, though we are through to the Greek camp, we're still a long way from victory. Most of your soldiers now seem more interested in looting and carrying off the spoils than fighting."

Even as they were speaking, just in front of them, an arrow from Teucer brought down the rugged Trojan spearman Imbrius. Anxious to claim the fallen man's armour as a trophy, Teucer charged forward. Hector flung his lance, but Teucer saw it coming and dodged out of its path.

The goddess Hera, seeing that Poseidon, ignoring Zeus' strict instruction not to interfere, had succeeded in rousing the Greeks, went to Mount Ida to join Zeus and divert his attention.

"Husband," she said softly, "you have been so busy lately, we have not had much time to be together."

"True," Zeus admitted. "Come to me now."

"Not here," protested Hera, "where all the gods and immortals can see us!"

"They won't see us," Zeus insisted, drawing a billowing, golden cloud around them.

Later, when Zeus was fast asleep, Hera crept away and summoned a messenger. She sent him straight to Poseidon, telling him to take advantage of Zeus' eyes being closed and whip up the Greeks to new heights of daring and bravery.

Receiving the word, Poseidon stung Idomeneus and his Cretan warriors into another attack and they began to cut a bloody swathe through the Trojan fighters.

Hector was still by the ramparts, trying to unseat Great Ajax, one man who was doing enough damage for a whole battalion. With tremendous force, Hector launched his spear at Ajax. But though it hit its target, the point struck where two sturdy leather straps crossed Ajax's chest and it failed to bring him down.

Ajax threw a boulder with all his might. The rock caught Hector on the neck with such force that it sent him crashing to the ground in pain.

Hordes of Greeks, hurling showers of spears, charged down the ramparts, hoping to drag Hector's stricken body off for the kill. But a ring of Trojan chiefs gathered round their leader and lifted him into a chariot, which sped off back to Troy.

The Anger of Zeus

When Zeus rose from his restful sleep, parted the clouds and looked down on the plain of Troy, he saw how badly the Trojans were doing now Hector was injured. Zeus was furious with Hera. "I thought I told you not to interfere?"

"And I didn't," she replied. "Your brother Poseidon decided all this for himself. He's the one who's been encouraging the Greeks."

Zeus, in a voice like thunder which could be heard all the way back to Mount Olympus, called for Iris. The messenger trembled before the great frowning Zeus, who instructed, "Go to my brother Poseidon and tell him to withdraw immediately. Either he must return to his palace beneath the sea, or come up here to discuss his actions with me. When that's done, I also want to talk to Apollo."

Iris, relieved to be away from Zeus, flew down to Poseidon and delivered his message. The sea-god was very angry. "What right has he to tell me what to do? Zeus and I are brothers and therefore equal. He can't order me about like one of his children."

Iris carefully suggested, "Perhaps you'd like to go up to Mount Ida and tell Zeus how you feel?"

At first she thought that Poseidon, whose face was as black as any thunder hurled by Zeus, would explode, but then he spluttered, "No, wait! Tell him that just this once, I will give way, for the sake of peace. But if he has any thought of sparing Troy, I will not agree and nor will Hera or Athena."

So saying, Poseidon angrily plunged down into the sea, sending wave upon wave crashing against the sides of the Greek ships. Iris was so relieved that as she flew to collect Apollo, she left a shimmering rainbow hanging in the sky.

The moment Apollo arrived, Zeus told him, "You must go to Hector and revive him. Heal his wounds and breathe new fire into him. Here, take my enchanted shield which has the power to protect you and Hector from

70

the Greeks. You two must stand at the head of the Trojan army and drive Agamemnon's troops as far as the ships. Go!"

Apollo found Hector, quickly helped him recover his strength, and then said, "Come, we must chase the Greeks back to their ships. I will go with you. My silver arrows never miss their target and I'll use my golden sword to cut a path through for you until the Greek warriors flee."

The Greeks, who had seen Hector dropped to the ground by Ajax, were shaken to see him back, unhurt, amongst his troops. Nor did they recognize the man beside him, whose shield fended off every lance, arrow, or stone they aimed at Hector.

But the sight put new heart into the Trojan warriors who forced the Greeks to beat a hasty retreat. With Apollo's help, Hector was soon crossing the trench, scaling the rampart and, moments later, clambering aboard the first captured Greek ship.

Waving his sword, Hector triumphantly declared, "Zeus has given us victory! Bring torches and we'll set fire to these ships which have brought us so much misery."

Flaming torches were hurled into the long wooden ship and soon it was ablaze.

A Brave Deception

The moment Patroclus saw the plumes of black smoke rising from the burning ship, he pleaded with Achilles, "Won't you take pity on us now? If you won't fight because of the prophecy, why not allow me to follow Nestor's plan and halt the Trojans by appearing before them wearing your armour?"

Achilles was stung by his friend's suggestion of cowardice. "Surely you don't imagine fear holds me back? Only Agamemnon's insult keeps me from being in the thick of battle. I told Odysseus and Ajax, I would not fight until I had to defend my fleet and the smoke you see is not coming from any of my ships! However, if you insist, I will lend you my armour and let you take our Myrmidon troops into battle. But, and remember this well, Patroclus, you must return once you have driven Hector's men from our camp. Whatever you do, don't advance on Troy. That prize is for me alone to take."

While Patroclus donned the splendid suit of armour King Peleus had given Achilles, the two immortal horses, Xanthus and Balius, were harnessed to Achilles' war chariot.

The Myrmidon warriors, tired of their enforced idleness and anxious to drive out the Trojans, needed no encouragement to put on their armour and take up their weapons.

Achilles watched them all go and then returned to his tent. Taking a two-handled golden cup, he poured himself some wine. Tipping some on the ground, he said, "Oh, Zeus, you have granted my wish that the Greeks should be driven back against their ships. Now grant me this next wish. I have sent my lifelong friend, Patroclus, into battle at the head of my Myrmidon troops. Give them the strength to show how courageous they are. That way, Hector will see what a great friend I have in Patroclus."

Ajax was growing tired from trying to defend the wooden decks. His head ached from the incessant blows his helmet was taking from Trojan arrows. His shoulders ached from the constant chopping and cutting he was forced to do to keep the Trojans back. His whole body was a river of sweat.

With his sword, Hector lunged at Ajax, slashing the point off his lance where the wooden shaft entered the socket, leaving it useless in Ajax's fist. Knowing the danger he was in without a spear, Ajax withdrew and soon another Greek ship was alight, the flames swiftly licking over the dry timbers.

Then Ajax heard a loud cry from the further end of the beach. Wearily he turned and was astonished to see someone who, judging by the armour, he took to be Achilles, leading a charge along the waterline. The marauding Trojan forces were being driven back from the ships.

Soon the Myrmidons, fresh and rested, were taking their toll of the battle-weary Trojan army.

"Look," the Trojans cried, "it's Achilles! The quarrel with Agamemnon must have been settled. Now he'll kill us all."

Even some of the Greeks were taken in by the deception, and it inspired them to join with the Myrmidons and help drive back the Trojans.

Patroclus hurled a spear into the fighters, who were milling round the stern of one ship. It hit Pyraechmes, slashing his right shoulder and dropping him to the ground. Seeing one of their best fighters killed, the Trojan soldiers around him began to scatter, terrified.

Wild as a storm sent down from Mount Olympus, the battle raged on.

Horse-riders were brutally dragged from their mounts and trampled to death by their own stallions. Dying charioteers had their skulls crushed under their own wheels.

A great cloud of dust was stirred up, as man fought man, and wherever the fighting was thickest, there was Patroclus with his Myrmidon warriors. At one point, as Patroclus pursued Hector, the team of immortal horses took his chariot right over the trench at a single bound.

Only the swiftness of Hector's horses, veering to one side, saved him from being overtaken.

But Patroclus made Pronous a victim of his spear, tearing open his chest above the rim of his shield. Next, he went for Thestor, who was crouching in fear in his chariot. Patroclus struck him with his spear with such force that Thestor was lifted dead from the chariot like a gaffed fish.

Sarpedon, seeing his Trojan allies dying around him, cried out, "I'll take him on myself and see who he is, this man who cuts the legs from under squads of our good brave men."

Patroclus and Sarpedon both leapt down from their chariots and squared up to each other.

Watching from above, Zeus, who knew full well who was wearing Achilles' armour, was horrified to see one of his sons facing up to Patroclus. But Hera cautioned Zeus, "Surely you don't want to save the life of a mere mortal? Well, do as you please, but beware, none of the other gods will respect you for it and soon they'll all be rescuing their sons from the battle! Many of those fighting down there are the sons of immortals. Dear as he is to you, leave Sarpedon to his fate and if he dies, then have his body returned to you."

Zeus knew that she was right, but that did not stop him shedding tears of blood over the boy.

Sarpedon threw his lance first, but it flashed by Patroclus and lodged in the shoulder of a horse. Screaming with pain, the horse crashed to the ground. Sarpedon hurled his second spear. It was a wasted shot, streaking by Patroclus without touching him.

But Patroclus did not miss. With his first spear he pierced Sarpedon in the stomach, spilling his guts on the ground.

When Sarpedon was down, Patroclus planted a heel on Sarpedon's chest

and tugged his weapon out, calling to his men, "He was one of the first men to storm our ramparts. Let's make an example of him. Strip him of his armour and slice him into shreds."

But the Trojans, guessing at what the Greeks intended to do to Sarpedon, charged forward and a violent combat broke out around his bloodied body.

Zeus watched, agonized, as he worked out the many different ways he could have Patroclus slaughtered. Should he let him be killed in the skirmish over his son's body? Of course, Patroclus was a friend of Achilles, that must be remembered too.

Zeus decided to start his plan with Hector, by turning Hector into a coward.

Hector immediately leapt into his chariot, crying out fresh orders, "Retreat, Trojans!"

The men obeyed and the Greeks could not stop themselves from chasing their enemy, leaving the trampled body of Sarpedon lying on the ground, forgotten.

But not by Zeus. "Go quickly," Zeus said to Apollo, "sweep Sarpedon clear of the weapons. Bathe him clean of blood, anoint him with oils and wing him away."

While Apollo was carrying out Zeus' orders, Patroclus, who had forgotten Achilles' words of caution, was urging his team of horses on towards Troy.

Three times he charged the city gates, but each time was repelled.

Hector pursued him, and Apollo saw the two were going to meet in single combat.

For the first time that day, Patroclus felt uneasy. Something moved by his shoulder but, as he turned to look, the unseen hand of Apollo knocked the helmet from his head.

Then a Trojan used the shaft of his spear to knock away Patroclus' spear. Patroclus rounded on his attacker but, in doing so, dislodged his shield strap, allowing the shield to fall to the ground.

As Patroclus bent to retrieve it, a young Trojan, Euphorbus, whose voice had not properly broken, croaked, "This is not Achilles!"

Suddenly, all fear gone, the young lad stuck his spear into Patroclus' back.

Patroclus, his face distorted with pain, staggered forward as he tried to

drag out the spear. With each tug he took another
step, and another, until Hector, seeing Patroclus
might escape, stepped forward and thrust a sword
into his side. Patroclus fell to the ground with a thud.

Hector straddled him. "Patroclus, did you think that by wearing Achilles'
armour you could frighten us all? Well, now your borrowed armour is
mine!"

Speaking with his dying breaths, Patroclus gasped, "It will do you no
good. You'll soon die at the hands of Achilles."

"If you're trying to frighten me with prophecies of death," Hector scoffed,
"it won't work. I'm not scared of Achilles. Let him come here now and I
will deal with him as I have with you!"

But Patroclus, lying dead in a pool of his own blood, could no longer
hear Hector's proud boast.

A Tide of Tears

From the moment the battle moved away from the ships, Achilles had been anxious for news of Patroclus and his men. As soon as he saw Nestor's son, Antilochus, hurrying towards him, Achilles knew all was far from well.

"Achilles," Antilochus gasped, "King Menelaus sent me to tell you that Patroclus is dead, killed by Hector near the city walls. When I left, they were still fighting over who should have the corpse, but Hector had already stripped him and taken your armour."

A wail of grief burst from Achilles' lips. "How can this be? I warned him not to venture near Troy, nor attempt to take on Hector."

"Your charioteer, Automedon, eventually managed to rescue your team. When the horses first saw Patroclus had fallen, they would not move, but stood over him, pawing the ground, with tears streaming from their eyes. I am sorry that I have brought you news I know you do not want to hear."

But Achilles, deep in mourning for his beloved friend, was not listening and Antilochus left quietly.

As soon as he was alone, Achilles released the bitter tears and let out a dreadful cry. Deep below the sea, in her silver cave, his mother heard his grief and cried out in turn. All the immortal sea-nymphs gathered round her, until the cave shimmered with them.

"Oh, my child!" Thetis wept. "Though I raised a flawless, mighty son, if he goes to battle now, I know that I will never have the chance to welcome him home again!"

She rushed to comfort him, emerging from the sea where the Myrmidons had beached their black ships. She found Achilles weeping in his tent and took his head in her arms. "My son, Zeus has done everything you wanted. What sorrow has touched your heart?"

"You are right," Achilles groaned. "Zeus brought to pass my heart's desire, but what joy is there in that now? Patroclus, my dearest friend, is dead! Hector has killed him and stripped him of the glorious armour I loaned him. Armour which Zeus presented to my father on your wedding day. Now I cannot rest until Hector is gasping his last breath. That's the blood-price for Patroclus, the gallant man he's killed."

"But remember," Thetis cautioned him through her tears. "Your death comes soon after Hector's."

"Then let that be sooner, rather than later," Achilles replied, "for, with Patroclus gone, I have lost the will to live. I have wasted all this time, nursing my anger against Agamemnon. But enough, what's done is done, it's time to avenge my friend's death."

"But how can you do that," Thetis asked, "when all your armour is in Trojan hands? Wait, I'll go now to Mount Olympus and talk to Hephaestus, the blacksmith of the gods. He will make you new and fabulous armour."

Hardly had Thetis gone, when Iris arrived. "Hera sent me to you. You must arm yourself straight away if you are to rescue the body of Patroclus. Between them, the Trojans and Greeks have been mauling it back and forth. Hector intends to drag it to Troy. He wants to remove Patroclus' head and display it on a stake, high on the walls."

"How can I go to battle," Achilles demanded, "while I have no armour?"

"Hera knows the fate of your armour," Iris replied. "She said, you must to the ramparts and show yourself. Just the sight of you may be enough to give the Trojans pause for thought and the Greeks time to escape with the body."

As soon as he had scaled the ramparts, Achilles saw Ajax trying to defend the battered body of his friend and, at the same time, fight off a horde of Trojans, who had gathered round him like jackals.

High above them, on the wall, Achilles let out a battle-cry, as loud as any trumpet. The Trojans, hearing his voice, began to quake. Three times Achilles let out the cry, holding them transfixed.

Ajax seized the chance to slip through the wall with the mutilated remains of Patroclus. Many hands lifted the body from the ground and placed him on a litter.

As the disappointed Trojans headed for home, Achilles joined the mourners and shed warm tears over the friend he had sent to war, but never welcomed home again alive.

Celestial Armour for Achilles

By dawn, Thetis returned to Achilles carrying a glorious new set of armour, which Hephaestus had forged in his smithy on Olympus.

The entire surface of the massive shield, which had been skilfully made from five layers of metal, was elaborately decorated with numerous scenes of earth, sky and sea. The greaves were of strong but pliable tin, while the well-formed breastplate gleamed brighter than burning fire and the sturdy helmet was topped with golden plumes.

Thetis laid the armour beside Achilles, who was still grieving over the loss of his friend. "My child," she said, "though it breaks your heart, you must leave your friend. See, I have brought you a gift from Hephaestus, god of fire. A finer set of armour no mortal has ever worn."

The Myrmidon soldiers shielded their gaze from the bright metal, but not Achilles. The glare of the sun glinting off the metal merely reflected the anger which was burning in his eyes.

As Achilles strode through the surf, he let out a cry which brought a host of others from the tents and ships. They all followed him to Agamemnon's tent, where the king lay, still recovering from his wound.

"King Agamemnon," Achilles said, "while I have been nursing my anger against you, too many of our friends have been killed. I have come to make amends, so that I may fight once more against the Trojans."

Agamemnon immediately replied, "I am relieved that all is well between us. The gifts Odysseus spoke of are still yours."

"I thank you," Achilles said graciously, "but I am more anxious to get my hands on the Trojans than your treasure."

"As an indication of your goodwill," Agamemnon suggested, "at least take back the girl Briseis, over whom we quarrelled."

"Very well," Achilles agreed. "But let us now go into battle."

Odysseus raised a hand. "Hold hard! The men have not yet eaten. You may be fresh and ready for battle, but they are tired and hungry."

"Go then, take your meal," Achilles answered, "the sooner we may get to war. I will take no food or drink till the sun goes down on this day."

While the men ate a breakfast of bread dipped in wine, and figs, Achilles returned to his tent with Briseis.

Without a word between them, she helped strap on Achilles' armour. Strong though the metal was, to Achilles the armour felt lighter than eagles' wings. He strapped on his silver studded sword and finally picked up his father's spear with its ash shaft, which no other fighter was strong enough to use. He went outside to find Automedon had already harnessed up Xanthus and Balius to his chariot.

Gently rubbing their velvety noses, Achilles spoke softly to them. "Soon we are going to fight Hector, but take care to gallop home fast. I don't want to fall into Trojan hands like Patroclus."

Both horses neighed and shook their manes and Xanthus said, "This time we'll bring you safely back, Achilles. But the day draws near when we can no longer help you. Even we cannot outrun the fate the gods have chosen for you."

"I know my own fate only too well," Achilles said impatiently, "but first Hector must pay the price for killing Patroclus!"

River of Blood

During a night of bitter argument, Hector had insisted that, if they were to face Achilles, they should do it out in the open. Polydamas, his close comrade, was positive their army would be too stretched if they fought so far from the city walls. He felt they had missed their opportunity to destroy the Greek ships and, now the quarrel with Agamemnon was over and Achilles was back in the fray, they ought to withdraw and concentrate on defending Troy.

But still swollen with pride over the death of Patroclus, Hector refused to listen to his friend's advice and vowed, "I'm not going to cringe like a frightened dog behind these walls. If Achilles wants his fill of fighting, I'll give it to him!"

So when Achilles, starved of war and hungry for revenge, led the Greek troops out on to the broad plain, he found the Trojan forces nervously awaiting him.

Without hesitation, Achilles led the charge and, with his Myrmidon army, began to hack through the Trojan ranks, slaughtering men to left and right. All day long they fought, slowly forcing the Trojans back to the banks of the River Scamander. Then Achilles drove them down into the water, where many perished, leaving the river running red with their blood.

But it was not until late afternoon, when what was left of the broken Trojan forces had withdrawn inside the city gates, that Achilles finally spotted Hector in the distance. He was standing alone before the Scaean Gate, clad in the armour he had taken from the dead body of Patroclus.

While the citizens of Troy ran in panic through the streets, King Priam and his wife stood on the gate tower, pleading with their son not to take on the mighty Achilles.

"Haven't I lost enough sons in this war?" Priam asked.

His mother, Hecuba, cried, "If you won't think of me, consider your wife and son!"

But nothing could shift Hector's resolve. "I cannot give way now. Last night Polydamas urged me to retreat, but I refused. Now I must face up to Achilles, or be dishonoured."

Some of Hector's courage began to fade, however, as Achilles drew nearer with his armour shining like fire. Hector wondered, if he disarmed himself and offered to negotiate a truce, would Achilles take Helen back and end the hostilities? That way, he could still emerge with his honour intact.

But Hector knew that if he appeared unarmed before Achilles, he would probably be slain in an instant. There was no way out, but to clash in battle!

Achilles, gripping his spear, never shifted his gaze from his quarry, as he strode on towards Hector.

At the last second, Hector's nerve failed and he began to tremble like a rabbit caught in the unswerving gaze of a fox. Hector could hold his ground no longer. Turning away from the gate, he fled in fear along the outside of the wall.

Achilles, known amongst the Greeks as the Great Runner, set off in pursuit.

Three times they circled the city. Three times they passed the wild fig tree and the bubbling springs which were the source of the River Scamander. Achilles stayed on the heels of his prey, as surely as any fox chases the rabbit and, just when Hector thought he might make a dash for the Dardan Gates, Achilles closed on him to drive him off.

As they started their fourth circuit, Hector suddenly stopped. "Enough!" he shouted to Achilles. "No more running from you in fear. My spirit stirs me to meet you face-to-face and I swear, if Zeus allows me to survive, once I've stripped your armour, I'll hand your body, unmutilated, to your colleagues."

Achilles laughed out loud. "I will make no pact with you, killer of Patroclus. Stand and fight!" And he hurled his massive spear at Hector.

But Hector saw the spear's long shadow hurtling towards him and dodged aside. "You missed! Now see if you can avoid my lance!"

Hector's spear struck the centre of Achilles' shield, but bounced off.

Achilles drew his sword and charged, looking for the weakest point in the armour Hector was wearing, his armour, which he knew so well. He remembered a spot, up near the throat, which had always needed careful guarding. Ducking through Hector's defences, Achilles caught Hector a slicing blow on the neck, watched the blood spurt out and Hector slide to his knees.

"Hah!" Achilles cried out in triumph. "When you killed Patroclus and stripped him of his armour, you thought you would be safe, never thinking his great avenger would strike you down in your turn."

Struggling for breath, Hector begged him, "Don't let the dogs devour me. My parents will give you gifts of gold and silver, if only you will allow my friends to carry home my body."

But, remembering the struggle which had gone on over his friend Patroclus' body, Achilles spurned his pleas. "Beg no more! There is not enough gold in the world to pay me to keep the dogs away from you. I'd sooner hack off your flesh myself and eat it raw!"

On the point of death, Hector hissed, "Achilles, your heart is made of iron. But now, beware, my curse is upon you! The day is close when Paris will destroy you before the Scaean Gate."

As Hector fell silent, Achilles began to rip the armour from the corpse. He slung it into his chariot, which Automedon had brought up alongside him. Then, while Hector's parents looked on in horror Achilles, bending over Hector's naked corpse, committed a terrible act of humiliation, so horrible it even sent shudders through the watching Greeks.

With his sword, Achilles cut a hole in both legs behind Hector's tendons, between ankle and heel. He threaded oxhide cords though the holes and lashed them to his chariot. Taking the reins from Automedon, Achilles whipped his horses and they sped off towards the Greek ships at a gallop, dragging the body of Hector behind them, face down in the dirt and rocks.

Funeral Games

So obsessed was Achilles that when they returned to camp he would not release the troops. "Before we take supper," he instructed, "stay in battle-order while we drive in honour past Patroclus."

Three times they drove round the body, Achilles still hauling Hector's corpse along in the dirt behind his chariot.

After the others had gone to unhitch their teams, Achilles stayed behind. "Farewell, Patroclus," he said, laying his hands on his friend's chest. "I've dragged Hector here for our dogs to rip him apart." Achilles untied Hector's battered corpse and flung it face down in the dirt beside Patroclus.

But when Achilles joined the others in Agamemnon's tent, he still refused refreshment of any kind. "I will take nothing," he declared, "until I have placed Patroclus on his funeral pyre and helped him make his final journey."

The following morning at first light, men set out in search of fuel. Driftwood was collected from the beach; they gathered the charred remains of some ships which Hector had set alight, and they hewed down living trees. Slowly, it was all built into a huge mound.

The men cut off lengths of their hair, which they laid on Patroclus as tokens of their affection. Then he was carefully lifted on to the pyre. Several dead sheep and goats were added, as offerings to the gods. At last, flaming torches lit the fire, which burned far into the night.

After the embers had been cooled with wine, men in tears carefully collected the ashes and bones of Patroclus, which they placed in a great gold urn.

Then Achilles addressed them all. "In honour of our comrade, I will offer the prizes for his funeral games."

Many races and trials of strength were arranged. There were archery contests, competitions for the best spear throwing and, most exciting of all, a chariot race.

When the games were over and everyone else had gone back to their camps with thoughts of food and sleep, Achilles sat alone, still grieving for his friend.

Thetis appeared beside him. "How long will you eat your heart out in torment? I bring a message from Zeus, who is angry with you for your monstrous treatment of Hector's body, which you, in your heartsick fury, still hold."

Achilles was surprised. "Have our dogs not eaten him yet?"

Thetis shook her head. "No, Aphrodite has been keeping them at bay and preserving his body. My son, you must give him back and take the ransom for the dead."

"Very well," Achilles agreed. "Tell Zeus, any Trojan who comes alone, and with a ransom, may take away the body."

Achilles and Priam

Zeus, pleased by Achilles' reply, sent Iris speeding to King Priam.

She found him wailing for his lost son and whispered, "Take heart, King Priam. Zeus commands you to ransom Hector, by bearing gifts to Achilles to soften his heart. But, apart from a trusted herald to drive the wagon for Hector's body, you must go alone. Yet fear not, Zeus will send a guide to lead you to Achilles and protect you from harm."

As Iris left, Priam ordered a wagon to be made ready, and summoned his chief herald, Idaeus.

But when his wife heard where Priam was going, she was horrified. "Are you mad? The moment Achilles has you in his clutches you will suffer the same fate as Hector!"

King Priam gently shook his head. "Hecuba, don't worry. If this message had come from a mortal man I wouldn't trust it. But if Zeus says I will be safe, then I must go and claim our son's body."

Once the wagon was loaded up with bars of gold, fine cauldrons and clothes cut from precious cloth for the ransom, Priam and Idaeus climbed aboard. Idaeus flicked the mules and they went out through the gates.

They were starting to cross the dark plain, when a mysterious figure, wearing winged, golden sandals, appeared hovering just ahead of them. "I am the god Hermes," he announced. "My father, Zeus, sent me to take you to Achilles."

He carefully led the way to the outskirts of the Greek camp, where he told them, "Achilles' tent is straight ahead, but I must leave you now. Remember to go in alone, then stir Achilles' heart by going down on one knee before him and reminding him of his own, ageing father."

With a whirr of his golden wings, Hermes returned to the heights of Olympus and Priam told Idaeus to wait with the mules.

When Priam entered Achilles' tent, Automedon had just finished serving supper and the table was still laden. The king slipped past Automedon and knelt before Achilles, clasping his knees and kissing his hands – the same hands which had killed Hector.

For a second, the two enemies stared in amazement at each other, finding it strange that, after ten years of the siege and all the many battles, they were at last standing so close to one another.

Using Hermes' advice, Priam earnestly prayed to Achilles, "Godlike Achilles, remember your own father, the noble King Peleus. He and I are much the same age. No doubt, while you have been so far from home, your father has worried over who will protect him. Of all my many sons, only Hector could guard Troy's walls and my people. Now you have killed him. I have come here tonight, bearing a ransom, to ask you to pity me and return his body to me."

Moved by his words, Achilles took Priam's hands. "Come, please, sit in this chair. What courage you have to dare to venture here tonight and amid all your sorrow. Let us put our grief to rest, each in our own hearts."

"Don't make me sit," Priam protested, "not while Hector lies uncared for in your camp. Take the ransom I have brought and give him back to me, now."

Achilles leapt to his feet. "Wait here," he instructed. "I will not keep you long."

He told Automedon to unload the ransom from the wagon, all save a fine cape and shirt. At the same time, he sent men to collect Hector's body. Briseis washed away the blood and dirt and anointed it with oil. Next they clothed it in the fine clothes Priam had brought and gently laid Hector in the wagon.

When Achilles returned to Priam, he spoke the words the old man most wanted to hear, "Your son is set free and now lies in state. Take food with me, and then set out at first light, in case Agamemnon sees you and questions the ransom."

Having rested, and just before daybreak, King Priam and Idaeus climbed aboard the wagon which bore Hector's body. "Just one more request, Achilles. I would like to give my son a truly royal burial. Give me twelve days to carry out that ceremony with dignity and then we'll fight again . . . if fight we must."

Achilles nodded and promised, "King Priam, it shall be as you ask."

As Priam was approaching Troy, word that he was returning with Hector's body spread quickly through the city. A crowd gathered by the gates and at the head of it, weeping bitter tears, were Hector's mother and his wife, Andromache.

"Dearest of all my sons!" cried Hecuba, as she knelt beside his body.

Andromache cradled his head. "Oh, my husband, cut off from life so young, leaving me a widow and your son, still a baby, orphaned!"

But there was a third woman, standing a little apart from the others, who also mourned for Hector. Helen, her beautiful eyes brimming with tears, sobbed, "Hector, dearest to me of all my husband's brothers! You never uttered one word against me but, oh, how I wish I had died before meeting Paris. That way he could not have brought me here to cause so much grief, and your death. In one breath I mourn for you and myself. For now there is no one left in the whole of Troy who will treat me kindly. All your countrymen cringe in loathing at the sight of me!"

During the days that followed, all the citizens of Troy went into mourning as the solemn ceremony of Hector's funeral took place. On the eleventh day, when the ashes of Hector's pyre had cooled, his remains were collected, shrouded in soft purple cloths and placed in a golden chest. The chest was lowered into a hole in the ground and the place marked with a large pile of carefully arranged stones.

And so the Trojans honoured Hector, perhaps their greatest hero.

Epilogue

ACHILLES AT THE SCAEAN GATE

With Hector dead, many of the Greeks believed the Trojans would not be able to hold out much longer and the war would soon be over. But that was not the case.

New allies rallied to the Trojan cause. Hundreds of brave women warriors, the Amazons, came on horseback, led by their renowned queen, Queen Penthesilea. King Memnon brought an army of Ethiopian soldiers.

Memnon took on Nestor's men and killed many of them, including Nestor's son, Antilochus. Nestor had watched in horror as Memnon drove his spear straight though the breastplate of Antilochus, stabbing him in the heart. But, before Nestor could claim his son's body, Memnon's men had forced the old man to retreat.

Nestor begged Achilles to rescue his son and Achilles, who had grown fond of Antilochus since the death of Patroclus, willingly agreed.

He fought his way through to the body, but found further advance blocked by the figure of Memnon, who heaved a rock at him. Achilles easily parried the rock with his shield and threw a spear, which caught Memnon's arm.

Drawing their swords, a furious fight developed, with both trying to gain the advantage and make a fatal strike. Eventually, with a massive thrust, Achilles caught Memnon a mighty blow, which crushed Memnon's breastplate into the bones of his chest.

As Memnon fell, Achilles led his troops in a charge towards the Scaean Gate, which the Trojans were struggling to close, amid hand-to-hand fighting.

Seeing victory within his grasp, Achilles threw aside his shield, grabbed a battle-axe and began to hack away at the woodwork.

High on the wall Paris, who had no taste for close combat, had a perfect view of the gate and of the damage Achilles was doing. Drawing an arrow from his quiver, he carefully picked his target and fired.

The arrow struck Achilles in the heel.

This was the heel by which his mother had held him as a baby, when she hoped to protect him by dipping him in the River Styx. But the special properties of the water had been unable to reach that one spot due to the tightness of his mother's grip.

Blood instantly spurted from the wound. Achilles, in tremendous pain, fell back as he struggled to tug out the offending barb.

"What coward dares shoot me only from behind?" Achilles roared with his last breath and then, with a great crash of his magnificent armour, he fell forwards into the gateway. The greatest of all Greek heroes was dead.

In the gateway, a furious battle developed over the body of Achilles but eventually Odysseus managed to lift him clear, get him to a chariot and back to his own tent in the Greek camp.

Briseis, her eyes filled with tears, washed Achilles' body and anointed him with oil. Men crowded round to place locks of their hair on his body and Thetis rose out of the sea to shed tears over her son, surrounded by her wailing sea-nymphs.

The Fall of Troy

Soon after the death of Achilles, Paris was also killed by an archer, one using a poison arrow. But still the siege did not end.

Finally, Odysseus came up with an idea which he believed might get the Greeks inside Troy's unyielding walls. He suggested they build a giant wooden horse with a hollow body, inside which he, together with a number of other soldiers, could hide. When it was built the Greeks left the horse standing on the plain, launched their wooden ships and rowed away.

The Trojans, believing the Greeks had, at long last, tired of the fruitless war and left them the horse as some sort of peace offering, went out to bring it inside the city walls. The horse was so large, they had to demolish part of one of the gates to get it through but, with the Greek soldiers gone, that no longer seemed important.

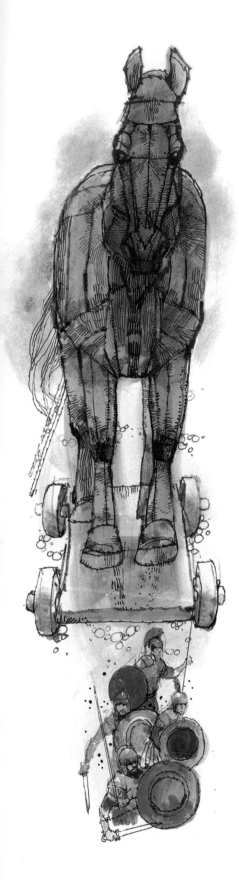

Eventually, the massive horse was hauled into Troy's main square, where it was greatly admired as the feasting began to celebrate the end of the long siege.

But the Greek ships had only gone a short distance along the coast. Under cover of darkness, they quietly returned to their moorings and the whole army crept up towards Troy where the citizens were sleeping off their revelry.

When the city was quiet, the Greek soldiers concealed in the horse's huge belly, led by Odysseus, Ajax and Menelaus, climbed out and silently slipped from house to house, slaughtering many Trojans in their beds. What few sentries were posted on the walls had had their throats slit by the time the main Greek force arrived. The city was thrown into panic as the Greeks poured through the streets, killing the Trojan men, taking the women and children prisoner, and looting every building, from house to palace.

Priam himself was murdered in the temple and the women of his household were added to the long line of other prisoners.

Once victory seemed certain, Menelaus set off, full of rage, searching for Helen. His intention had been to kill her for betraying him, but when he found her, sitting all alone, deserted by everyone, pity began to stir memories of their life together, before Paris had taken her away. Helen, surrounded by the dreadful results of her actions, lowered her head in shame as she walked towards him.

As the Greeks left with their captives, they set fire to the city. Looking back from the plain, Queen Hecuba, who was walking in chains with the other women, remembered the dream she had experienced before the birth of Paris, which foretold how her beloved city would finally be destroyed by flames.

Next day, with their ships weighed down with treasures and prisoners, the Greeks set off for the homes they had not seen for so long.

All of the prophesies of the gods had been fulfilled and what had started as a trivial quarrel between three jealous goddesses over who should have the golden apple, had led to a bitter war, causing much pain and misery, in which countless men from both sides lost their lives. But the heroes and victims, both Greek and Trojan, will never be forgotten.

Glossary of Characters

The Greeks and their Allies

Achilles (*a-kil'-eez*): son of Peleus and Thetis, commander of the Myrmidons
Agamemnon (*a-ga-mem'-non*): king of Mycenae, brother of Menelaus
Ajax (*ay'-jax*)
Antilochus (*an-ti'-lo-kus*): son of Nestor
Automedon (*aw-to'-me-don*): charioteer of Achilles and Patroclus
Calchas (*kal'-kas*): prophet, son of Thestor
Chiron (*keye'-ron*): a Centaur, friend of Achilles and Peleus
Diomedes (*deye-o-mee'-deez*): king of Argos
Eurypylus (*yoo-ri'-pi-lus*): king of Cos
Helen (*he'-len*): daughter of Zeus, wife of Menelaus, consort of Paris
Idomeneus (*eye-do'-men-yoos*): commander of Cretians
Machaon (*ma-kay'-on*): co-commander of Thessalians
Menelaus (*me-ne-lay'-us*): husband of Helen, brother of Agamemnon
Nestor (*nes'-tor*): king of the Pylians
Odysseus (*o-dis'-yoos*): warlord of Ithaca
Patroclus (*pa-tro'-klus*): friend of Achilles
Peleus (*peel'-yoos*): father of Achilles, king of the Myrmidons
Teucer (*tyoo'-sur*): master-archer

The Trojans and their Allies

Agastrophus (*a-gas'-tro-fus*)
Andromache (*an-dro'-ma-kee*): wife of Hector
Aeneas (*ee-nee'-as*): son of Aphrodite, commander of the Dardanians
Antenor (*an-tee'-nor*): counsellor to Priam
Antiphus (*an'-ti-fus*): son of Priam
Bienor (*bi-ee'-nor*)
Briseis (*breye-see'-is*): daughter of Briseus, captive of Achilles
Cassandra (*ka-san'-dra*): daughter of Priam
Charops (*ka'-rops*): brother of Socus
Chersidamas (*kur-si'-da-mas*)
Chryseis (*kreye'-see-is*): daughter of Chryses, captive of Agamemnon
Chryses (*krye'-seez*): priest of Apollo, father of Chryseis
Coon (*koh'-on*): son of Antenor

Dolon (*doh'-lon*): Trojan scout
Ennomus (*en'-o-mus*): co-commander of the Mysians
Euphorbus (*yoo-for'-bus*)
Glaucus (*glaw'-kus*): co-commander of the Lycians
Hector (*hek'-tor*): son of Priam and Hecuba, supreme commander of the Trojans
Hecuba (*he'-kew-ba*): wife of Priam, mother of Hector
Helenus (*he'-le-nus*): son of Priam
Idaeus (*eye-dee'-us*): herald of Priam
Imbrius (*im'-bri-us*)
Iphidamas (*eye-fi'-da-mas*): son of Antenor
Isus (*eye'-sus*)
Memnon (*mem'-non*): king of the Ethopians
Odius (*od'-i-us*): co-commander of the Halizonians
Pandarus (*pan'-da-rus*): commander of forces from Zeleaz
Paris (*pa'-ris*): son of Priam and Hecuba
Penthesilea (*pen-the-sil-ee'-a*): queen of the Amazons
Phaestus (*fees'-tus*): Trojan ally
Phegeus (*fee'-joos*)
Polydamas (*po-li'-da-mas*)
Priam (*preye'-am*): king of Troy, father of Hector and Paris
Pronous (*pro'-no-us*)
Pyraechmes (*peye-reek'-meez*): commander of the Paeonians
Rhesus (*ree'-sus*): Trojan ally
Sarpedon (*sar-pee'-don*): Trojan ally
Scamandrius (*ska-man'-dri-us*)
Socus (*soh'-kus*): brother of Charops
Sthenelus (*sthe-ne-lay'-us*)
Thestor (*thes'-tor*)
Thoon (*thoh'-on*)

The Gods

Aphrodite (*a-fro-deye'-tee*): goddess of love, mother of Aeneas
Apollo (*a-pol'-oh*): god of the Sun
Ares (*ai'-reez*): god of war
Athena (*a-thee'-na*): goddess of war and wisdom
Hephaestus (*he-fees'-tus*): god of fire
Hera (*heer'-a*): queen of the gods
Hermes (*hur'-meez*): messenger of the gods
Iris (*eye'-ris*): messenger of the gods
Poseidon (*po-seye'-don*): god of the sea
Thetis (*the'-tis*): sea-goddess, wife of Peleus, mother of Achilles
Zeus (*zyoos*): king of the gods